Here's What Readers Of Advance Copies Of The *96 Billion Dollar Game: You Are Losing* Had To Say

"With a legal career that was immersed in all sides of the litigation process, and with an impressive mass of conscientious and genuine research to draw upon, author Phil Hermann is able to find and suggest the most prudent path for each of the players" in the 96 Billion Dollar game of injury reimbursement. Every facet of the game is exposed and explained in this book. It could serve as a strategic tool for anyone remotely involved in our negligence recovery system. His disclosure that the customary methods used in the negotiation and settlement are wasting time and money for everyone, makes it profitable reading for both the "givers" and the "takers" in this highly economic game."

ELMER P. SIMON, Chairman (retired)
F.M. Mutual Insurance Company

"I have read *The 96 Billion Dollar Game.* Its excellent scholarship and splendid portrayal of a lifetime of 'playing game' should be of interest and should be a rewarding experience for anyone interested in lawyers or personal injury litigation. I enjoyed the chance to read your book."

LYLE W. ALLEN, Past President
Illinois State Bar Association

"I believe the book will give the general public an insight as to impact of our business on their daily lives and particulary their pocketbooks...while the more sophisticated professionals--both legal and insurance--should know how the personal injury game is played and how they can tilt the playing field to their advantage, your work would serve as a useful primer to those entering these professions or who do not deal with personal injury matters on a regular basis. In effect, the book would be an excellent introduction to the real world of personal injury litigation and provide the reader with what he or she never learned in the academic world of law school and/or college."

JOSEPH P. MONTELEONE, Sr. VP Claims
Reliance National

"Enjoyed reading Phil's latest book. I found it very helpful."

ARCHIE ROBINSON, Past President
D.R.I.

THE 96 BILLION DOLLAR GAME YOU ARE LOSING

How Personal Injury Litigation Has Become A Costly Game To You

BY

Philip J. Hermann

IF YOU

Purchase Automobile, Casualty, Malpractice Insurance, Are Injured, Sued, Are An Insurer Or Self-Insurer, A Lawyer Who Handles Personal Injury, A Taxpayer, Purchase Products, Or Use Services That Can Injure People.

HOW TO TAKE CONTROL AND SAVE BIG

LEGAL INFORMATION PUBLICATIONS, INC.
23811 Chagrin Blvd., LL 42
Beachwood, OH 44122

Cover Designed By:

Michelle Brown

Library of Congress Cataloging: 92-075680
ISBN Number: 0-9635375-1-2

The 96 Billion Dollar Game: You Are Losing.
Author Philip J. Hermann

Editorial support: Andrew Hamilton, Louis Oswald
Marcia Cuyler-Lewis

This book is distributed by Publishers Distribution Services, 121 E. Front St., Suite 203, Traverse City, MI 49684. 800-345-0096

FOREWORD

Judge Lambros

For anyone who has ever wondered why the insurance premiums on their automobile, business or profession are so high, for every injured victim who endured a long wait for compensation, for anyone who has been sucd and suffered years of anxiety before their insurance company settled the claim, this book will serve to enlighten, educate and assist. For the automobile and casualty insurance executive, whose company is losing millions of dollars, the business person who isn't making money on a product line or feels apprehensive about introducing a new one for fear of litigation and the attorney who watches his legal fees being eaten up in litigation costs, this book will show what can be done to stem the tide of loss.

The problem that we as a society face today is the common perception that litigation through verdict is the only way to achieve fair compensation for an injury. The conventional wisdom holds that the closer to verdict a case gets, the more money is likely to be proffered. The basic flaw in this rationale is that it fails to take into account the economics of getting a case to the point of verdict. Personal injury litigation has simply become too expensive and time consuming to achieve the goal of fair compensation in all cases. This is not to say that all litigation is without merit. Of course, there will always be cases where litigation is not only necessary, but productive as well.

However, a vast majority of common injury claims today are not well served by the litigation process. When the facts surrounding liability are clear and the offer and demand are within reason, such cases should be settled promptly before they enter the quagmire of litigation and the attendant costs. In this book, Mr. Hermann deftly illustrates the net effect if prompt settlement on all of the participants. By examining the economics of the typical injury case, Hermann demonstrates the true cost of litigation through verdict and compares this with the earning potential of an early settlement. By exploring such factors as inflation, lost interest and investment potential, Hermann graphically depicts just how beneficial prompt settlement can be for all parties concerned. Throughout the text, Hermann remains impartial and offers sound advice for plaintiff and defense counsel as well as the insurers and the injured. I have spent the better part of my life, first as an insurance adjuster, later as an attorney representing both the injured and insurance companies and eventually as a judge, in trying to bring the opposing parties in tort cases to a common ground. As a Common Pleas Judge for the State of Ohio for over six years, and as a U.S. District Court judge for the past 26 years, I look upon the tort compensation system in America as a fair and just system where individuals as well as companies are held accountable for their negligence and where injured victims receive their day in court. It is a system where juries decide who is at fault and how much the injured victim should be compensated. The guiding principle behind the system is to discourage acts of negligence while attempting to make the injured victim whole again.

Mr. Hermann is not offering a panacea for the perceived ills of our tort compensation system nor is he advocating tort reform or new legislation. What Phil presents in this book are practical solutions that will help minimize the cost and delays typically associated with personal injury litigation while ensuring prompt and equitable compensation for the injured at a minimum cost to the insurer. I consider this book a must for all to read.

Honorable Thomas D. Lambros
Chief Judge
U.S. District Court
Northern District of Ohio

PREFACE

THE 96 BILLION DOLLAR GAME

Justice is never cheap, but the system that we now have is ridiculous.

This book tells us why. Those who think they are or will be winners are not. While the innocent incur enormous expenses to prove their innocence. And this happens while the system draws resources away from providing simple justice and instead stifles efficiency, maximized transaction costs and sows the seeds of disrespect.

The civil justice reform movement is now in full bloom; it is yielding an amazing array of colorful proposals for reform. This book thus belongs to a distinguished genre of ever expanding information about what has gone wrong. But this book is distinctive. It does not seek to identify a single villain. The fault is not solely in the hands of avaricious plaintiffs lawyers, or foot dragging defense lawyers. It is not in the hands solely of overworked judges. Similarly, the book does not seek to advocate a specific reform or push a political agenda.

The focus of the book is straightforward--the problem is not with people, but with information they have to work with. The problem is not with the system, but with the lack of insight about what will make the system work better. The remedy is not systemic reform, but the positive value of showing each player in the litigation struggle that their self-interest is advanced by finding a better approach. The insight in this book will lead each player towards a better understanding of how to use the system we have more effectively and will therefore, lead to more justice at less cost.

Dean Peter M. Gerhart
Case Western Reserve University
School of Law

CONTENTS

Part I **The High Stakes Game**

1. You Are Playing a High Stakes Game Without Knowing It and Losing Big 1

2. How Did Personal Injury Litigation Become a Game? 6

3. The Bankroll: A $96 Billion Dollar Pot 15

4. The Opening Bet: Insurers Gamble 40% of Your Premiums 27

5. Policyholders May Never Play a Hand, But They Pick up the Tab 50

6. Victim Again: The Injured Lose $9 Billion 61

7. Raising The Bet: Plaintiff Attorneys Risk $7.5 Billion 73

8. The High Rollers: Defense Lawyers Play a Loose Game 85

9. The Side Bet: Self-Insurers' $18 Billion 87

10. Hoyle's Rules: Billion-Dollar Juries With Final Say 90

Part II **The Kibitzers and Players Blame Each Other, But Overlook the Reason That Litigation Has Become a Costly Game: Substitution of the Partially Educated Guess for Information and Marketing**

11. Beefing Up the Pot: Expensive Trials and Clogged Court Dockets 94

12. The Scam: 85 Percent Play Losing Hands 111

13. The Politics: Casting Aspersions, Each Player Overlooks His Bad Plays 119

14. Playing Without the Hole Card: The Partially Educated Guess Dominates the Negotiating Charade 128

15. Public Officials Who Promise You Lower Insurance Premiums Through Rate Regulation Are a Major Cause of the Game 149

Part III **The Practical Steps That Players Can Take to Change the Costly Game into a Cost-Effective Business**

16. Betting The Odds: Jury Information Leads to Fair Settlement 153

17. The Ace In The Hole: Information 166

18. The Wild Card: Marketing 177

Part IV **Taking Control**

19. How to Take Control and Save Big 187

20. Sued: You are the Central Character in the Game 189

21. Policyholders: The Winning Hand Can Be Yours 194

22. Insurance Executives: You Can Deal Yourself a Winning Hand 203

23. The Self-Insured: You Are a Major Player 225

24. The Injured: To Keep From Being a Victim Again, Keep Your Eye on the Pot 226

25. Lawyer (For The Injured): You Can Win a Bigger Pot for Your Client and Yourself 229

26. The Defense Attorney: You Can Help Reduce the Pot 232

27. The Judge (Also the Arbitrator): You Can Play a Leading Role in Ending this Game 237

28. You! The Law Maker Regulator: Sponsor This Game 238

29. The Final Play: Information, Marketing and Economics Can Force an End to Non-productive Litigation 240

APPENDIX 241

#1

You're Playing A High Stakes Game Without Knowing It And Losing Big

In 1991, you contributed your share of over $96 billion in litigation! How much you contributed depends upon who you are and what you do. Your share can be in the thousands, or the hundreds of thousands of dollars. Worse yet, your share increases each year! Almost everyone over the age of twenty-one is playing the game.

The game is personal injury litigation as it is practiced today.

Why do I call it a game? Almost everyone involved loses, many lose big. Most of those who think they've won, have actually lost! With such dismal results and gigantic costs, what can personal injury litigation be called except a game! Can anyone who critically examines personal injury litigation today, its costs, how little it accomplishes, call it a rational endeavor?

If you own and insure an automobile, home, property, or a business, you are paying a lot more than you should in insurance premiums. If you are a stockholder, your loss may be similar but indirect and reflected in smaller earnings and dividends.

If you purchase any product or service that can injure someone (and most products can), you are paying what can best be described as a litigation tax. Everything you buy is priced to cover litigation, past, present and future.

If you get seriously ill, a large chunk of the medical costs you incur will be for litigation. Whether you travel, stay in a hotel, or attend a sporting event, part of your charges include litigation costs.

A portion of your taxes go for litigation, which pay for the judges, their staffs, and the courtrooms.

When adding up the different ways unnecessary personal injury litigation is costing, you will be dismayed at how large the cost is.

If you work for wages and own a car, a house, buy modestly, and use services carefully, the cost to you can be at least a thousand dollars a year. Even a person with greater income, in business or the professions, you are losing thousands. The cost to business of size is much more.

If you are sued, your litigation costs can become even more formidable, though you are insured. Insurance usually does not pay for your loss of income or your expenses to attend legal proceedings. These proceedings are often many and time consuming. They include meetings with your attorneys; preparing and gathering information, depositions and interrogatories, pre-trials, preparation for trial, and waiting in your attorney's office or courtroom to start the trial. These legal processes may be topped off by a trial that lasts for weeks. If you are a wage earner, the additional costs can be in the hundreds of dollars. If you are a professional, your additional losses can be much more. If your business is sued, your additional losses can be in the tens of thousands of dollars. Each year your litigation costs continue to skyrocket.

Some litigation can kill the success of a new meritorious product or your whole business! Litigation may prevent the introduction of important products, such as a new drug that could save your life!

Personal injury litigation that benefits one side or the other is important to asserting and preserving important rights. However, litigation that benefits neither the claimant nor the defendant is non-productive. A claimant is anyone who makes a claim. In this book, this person is also called the injured and the plaintiff.

Most personal injury litigation fails to help anyone, including the injured on whose behalf the litigation originates, or the insurance company which defends against the claim. Evidence shows that approximately 85 percent of personal injury litigation serves no useful purpose. Other forms of litigation may serve better or worse. However, since this book deals only with personal injury litigation, I will simply call it litigation.

Since 85 percent of litigation serves no useful purpose, it can only be called a game. In fact, it is played as a game.

A lawsuit is often filed not because the offer is unfair or the demand is too high. Litigation is often started because of a lack of knowledge of what the injury is worth. Neither side may bother to find out what it's worth, though such information is available. They want to see who blinks first...whether the insurance company will pay more or the claimant take less. In 90 percent of litigation, one side blinks and settlement occurs.

This may not happen until years of costly litigation, frequently in the courtroom. Often, the settlements or verdicts are similar to the demand or offer made before filing suit.

Where the verdict or settlement is much larger, the net to the claimant is often less. After deducting additional expenses, lost interest, and inflation that decreases what the money will buy.

Where the insurance company finally pays much less than the demand made before litigation, its total costs are often much more. Defense costs are also high.

Fewer than three percent of the claims filed in court go through trial to a verdict. Even here the game continues. Often spurning a sizable offer, the injured litigant, on his lawyer's advice, rolls the dice, hoping to get a lot more. The odds are stacked against this happening. In 37 to 40 percent of all cases, the jury awards the claimant nothing! Another 11 percent are awarded less than $10,000 and ten percent receive between $10,000 and $50,000. Actually, with some exceptions, juries are surprisingly conservative.

The insurance carrier will frequently turn down a reasonable settlement demand only to be greeted with a verdict many times larger.

When the jury awards the injured nothing or less than the final offer, plaintiff's counsel will blame the jury and judge. Actually, he didn't do his homework. Plaintiff's counsel should have known from past jury decisions how the jury would render their verdict.

Often the award is much larger than the final demand. Defense counsel will blame a runaway jury--a jury that gives away defendant's money and, of course, the judge is blamed. The insurance company and defense counsel didn't do their homework either!

Why those who control settlement and litigation prefer to play a game without bothering to know their hole card is mind-boggling. Unfortunately, they not only penalize the injured but you as well.

To gain control of this game, you must understand what the game is all about, why litigation has become a game and the role of the many participants in this game--including you. This book tells you how to gain control and save big.

#2

How Did Personal Injury Litigation Become A Game?

Personal injury litigation is out of control. It has become a game with a $96 billion a year ante that most everybody loses. Some authorities claim the annual cost is 300 billion.

How did personal injury litigation become a game? Like so many problems, it didn't happen overnight. And there are many to blame.

When I entered the practice of law 50 years ago, personal injury litigation was a serious pursuit. Usually, only occurring if there was a strong disagreement as to fault, injury or law.

Most claims were settled directly by the insurance company adjuster, with few claimants hiring lawyers. If the lawyer consulted didn't specialize in personal injury, he referred the claim to an attorney who did. The result was a personal injury professional representing the injured and a personal injury professional representing the insurance company. If the claim manager could not settle the claim, he called in their defense counsel.

Most claims were settled without a lawsuit being filed. As defense counsel, most of my defense litigation originated from a handful of law firms that specialized in representing the injured.

Then a big change occurred. Attorneys representing the injured formed a national bar association that is now called The Association of Trial Lawyers of America (ATLA). When attorneys began to recognize that the scope of law was expanding fast, to keep up with developments required them to attend seminars. All bar associations rose to the challenge, including ATLA.

Attorneys also began to recognize that personal injury generated large fees. So they flocked to the ATLA seminars conducted by the nation's foremost trial lawyers in representing the injured.

Soon, many of the attorneys consulted by the injured decided they did not need to share the fees they received from personal injury cases. They decided they had learned enough to negotiate settlements. Many of these attorneys began using litigation as a substitute: Since their knowledge of personal injury cases, law, and their stature did not compare with the masters, they reasoned that at pre-trial a kind judge would help them out. Unfortunately, the first pre-trial may not happen until months or years after a suit is filed. If the case didn't settle and was heading for the trial room, a specialist in personal injury trials was brought in. This may have been years after the case entered into litigation. Many trial specialists, after reviewing the situation, would not agree to handle the case. Thus, the attorney without trial experience had a problem. He could settle the case for whatever he could get or do his best at trying the case.

With the public realizing that they could financially benefit from all kinds of personal injury cases even for those without merit, more and more claimants flocked to all kinds of attorneys. After the United States Supreme Court authorization of attorney advertising, this became a flood.

Before blaming so-called money-hungry claimants and lawyers, I have only given you a prelude to litigation becoming a game. There are many more participants in making personal injury into a game.

When a person is injured, and it is someone else's fault, agreeing on fair compensation becomes an important decision in that person's life. Yet, the claimant is given less information than is contained on the label of a can of soup. The insurance adjuster starts by telling the injured how much the company will pay. You would not buy a can of soup without knowing more than the price. Yet, an insurance agent of that company appears with various charts and actuarial information, including the estimated cash value of the policy at different years, and the interest rate, in case you want to borrow money on the insurance policy. The agent will clearly point out why his policy is superior to the competitors.

While the life insurance agent is providing information and engaging in marketing, the insurance adjuster, on the other hand, is simply playing a game.

Wearing a big smile, the adjuster will tell the injured how much the company will pay. When the claimant asks how he is supposed to know if the offer is fair, the adjuster provides the same response that a poker player would give, a trusting smile. The game is similar to stud poker. The adjuster expects the claimant to decide to call without knowing his own hole card.

Does the adjuster tell the injured what amount he can expect from a jury? If so, how much will he net? Is the claimant told how long of a wait to expect? Has the claimant been told how the offer, plus the interest earned, compares to the probable verdict? The answer is usually **NO!** If the injured balks at playing the game, the adjuster may simply raise the bet. Obviously, the insurance adjuster has yet to become a member of either the information, or the marketing age.

This book zeros in on why the adjuster fails to negotiate reasonable settlements with the injured. It also provides practical information on how the insurance company can settle most of their claims without overpaying or losing control to an attorney and needless litigation.

Over half of the people who file claims and over 80 percent of those with serious injuries run to another player; the lawyer, when they don't trust the adjuster's game.

Unfortunately, the lawyer also may play a game of high-stakes poker with the client. The hole card may still be hidden. Too often, the lawyer has no idea of what the injured can expect at the hands of a jury. However, the lawyer, does have a standard play when facing the injured's questions about the fairness of the offer: the claimant is told "the adjuster's offer is ridiculously low, I will get you much more! To get the insurance company to pay the full price, they must be sued".

Now, the game starts in earnest with pleadings, motions and depositions. Months pass, and the only action has been the taking of the injured's deposition and a few meetings with counsel. The claimant discovers, to his amazement that he is not the star player, though it is his future that is at stake.

The plaintiff (this is how the claimant is referred to in court) doesn't get any phone calls or letters from his attorney. His phone calls may not be returned. Upon further prodding, his lawyer's secretary informs him that the court docket is jammed. The case must wait its turn.

Months or even years later, the game resumes with a pre-trial hearing before a judge. This brings in the next player, the judge. However, the judge may not be any better informed. Instead of being of any real help, the judge too plays poker with a blind hole card. Very little, if anything, happens. The offer may go up some. The claimant's attorney will insist that it's still much too low. The company will only bid its true hand in the courtroom and the injured player begins to realize the frustration of this time-consuming game. A game where each new hand can take years.

Then one day, as the lawyer prepares his client for trial; he discovers that he is an important person after all. The claimant discovers for the first time, there is a chance the jury may not award him any money. Equally disturbing, the lawyer also confides to his client: by the luck of the draw, they have drawn a judge whose juries have been stingy and unpredictable.

Although the information is available, the injured still hasn't been told his chances of winning this game, or the probable verdict amount if successful. The claimant is a player with little information except the current offer, and the disturbing knowledge that he may lose altogether.

The judge may suggest to the plaintiff to take the latest offer, but provides no helpful information. Sympathetic that they have been dealt a bad hand, namely, this judge, the claimant's lawyer may suggest that under the circumstances it would be best to accept the offer and end the game.

The claimant discovers that his share after expenses and attorney fees may be only a little more, and sometimes even less, than what was offered years ago. The injured party will leave the courtroom unhappy with the settlement.

On the other hand, the claimant and his attorney may still want to hold out for a larger pot. If so, they will play the game to the bitter end.

With few exceptions, the jury's verdict may be the last disappointing hand. In the game that was played, the injured thought that jurors were generous with insurance company money. The claimant was not told that in 37 to 40 percent of the cases they hear, jurors award nothing. Or when they do award money, 15 percent of the plaintiffs get less than $10,000 and 27 percent get between $10,000 and $50,000. Even when a large sum of money is awarded, it is often less than the final offer. The claimant is finally beginning to realize that even gamblers in Las Vegas have better odds of winning.

If the jury is generous, the game is extended. Additional legal moves are used in an attempt to take away part or all of the winnings. Years after the game began, the claimant may have to settle for less than the jury awarded him. Then, after deducting out-of-pocket expenses, and attorney fees, the claimant is dismayed at how much further his long awaited pot-of-gold has shrunk.

The full frustration and expense of this game is understood when the claimant realizes that if a reasonable offer had been accepted and invested earlier; it may have grown too many times the size of the final net settlement or verdict.

Unfortunately, this game is not only frustrating, but very expensive to all the players.

Policyholders, insurance companies, defendants, taxpayers,

defense attorneys and plaintiff lawyers all pay the price. The injured's lawyer may sadly discover he did not cover his overhead costs.

The ante is an estimated $96 billion a year. Yet, the players are so obsessed with litigation as the solution to their problems that few ever sit back to examine this expensive, self-defeating game.

Ninety percent of all personal injury lawsuits are settled without the help of a jury. With few exceptions, these cases simply should have never entered litigation. Even a high portion of the three percent submitted to juries should have been settled or withdrawn.

If an alien from outer space was observing the personal injury game, he would be flabbergasted by it. In a system where a jury decides if the injured is entitled to compensation and if so how much, few of the players bother to find out what jurors do.

Information on jury outcome is readily available and has been for many years. It shows that jurors with some exceptions are consistent when ruling whether or not the injured is entitled to collect.

Furthermore, jurors with exceptions are surprisingly consistent in their awards, when the injuries and economic losses are similar. Yet, most of the players play blindfolded. As a result, we have a $96 billion game that few win.

This book shows the players that by getting and using important information, they can remove the blindfolds with justice to all players. The adjuster can show the attorney that significant sums of money can be lost by resorting to needless litigation and visa versa. The attorney can get the best settlement by showing the adjuster how litigation is sure to drive up defense costs. The judge can clear his docket by proving to each party with the information provided that litigation is counterproductive.

The sole purpose of litigation is to help resolve a wrong. If it does not, it serves no purpose. To this end, litigation does have an important role in personal injury .

If the claimant is not offered what a jury can be expected to award (minus expenses), he is justified in suing to obtain equitable compensation. If the claimant wants more than a jury would probably award, the insurer is justified in defending its interest through litigation.

Determining who is at fault, or deciding whether the law entitles the victim to be compensated are serious questions. These may have to be resolved by the courts. Surprisingly, most of these cases are settled by compromise.

In some situations, lawyers need information about the incident or injury. Information that can only be obtained through depositions, and other legal processes. Many of these cases can be settled shortly after such information is secured, and questions are resolved. There is often no reason for letting a case continue through this expensive court process, but most do.

However, most litigation results because the players have not entered the information and marketing age.

An estimated 85 percent of all litigation expense could be eliminated if the players simply would enter the information and marketing age. Of the 15 percent, at least two-thirds of them should settle as soon as the litigants have discovered the facts needed to determine what the case is worth. This is usually within months. However, litigation feeds upon itself. Some cases have been needlessly pending for years.

Once the policyholders, attorneys, insurers, litigants, and judges see the enormous cost to play this game, and realize how they got into the mess, they will join the information and marketing age out of self-interest. Everyone will benefit.

In the next chapter, we examine how the pot became $96 billion.

#3

The Stakes: A $96 Billion Dollar Pot

Whether they are playing the game or not, personal injury litigation reaches the pocketbook of just about every American. From the factory worker insuring a new Ford, to the Chief Executive Officer insuring a billion-dollar manufacturing firm, the policyholders and insurance companies are not the only ones who pay. There are millions of others involved: the injured public, their attorneys, the defense attorneys, the juries, even the taxpayers who pay the judge's salary. Further removed, but still paying, are the consumers who get stuck with higher prices because of the costs passed on by manufacturers, transportation companies, doctors and retailers.

Altogether, about $96 billion is spent in the litigation of personal injury lawsuits in this country each year. That is $386 for every man, woman and child in the country. What is shocking, is that this money is not spent to compensate the injured, but to litigate their cases.

No one objects to fairly compensating a person who has been hurt as a result of someone else's carelessness. However, when the applicable law, the facts of the case, or even the cause of the injury are not clear, problems and often litigation arise. To guide society through the intricacies of who pays what, the laws of negligence or torts have evolved.

Torts are wrongful acts that cause personal injury or property damage for which the law provides redress. They arise out of just about any situation, but auto accidents are by far the most common cause of injuries. There were over

33,370,000 million motor vehicle accidents resulting in 5,560,000 million injuries in the U.S. in 1990, according to the Insurance Information Institute. However, that's only the beginning.

Careless medical treatment can prompt a medical malpractice claim. In New York City, a 41 year old subway car mechanic went to the emergency room twice with pain in his calf. The emergency room doctors treated him for skin and vein inflammations and sent him home. The man died of an embolism a few days after the second visit. At the trial, five years later, the jury awarded the family $1,565,000. The parties settled for $1,300,000 after the trial.

Building owners can be held liable for hazardous conditions at apartments, shopping centers, office buildings, playgrounds, sidewalks and just about any public place. At a 1991 trial, a young mother claimed that she had repeatedly asked her landlord to remove the lead paint from her apartment, but he never responded. Her three year old son ate the paint chips and contracted lead poisoning. The jury's verdict was for $2.6 million.

There are many types of situations that cause injury: defective products, inadequate security at hotels and motels, false arrests by police and security guards, inadequate warnings on products or at dangerous areas, wrongful employee firings, delinquent legal representation, inattentive bartenders, unconstrained pets...the list is endless. The injury is not always as dramatic as the dead patient or the brain-damaged baby. Although, they cover the full spectrum of possibilities: quadriplegia, bruises, mental incapacitation, and the inability to sleep, the resulting jury award is most often not in the millions.

A typical case is the one involving a 21 year old Nebraska man who was changing his tire by the side of the road. When his car was hit by another vehicle, his back was hurt and he sued the driver of the other car. A jury awarded him $3,700 two years after the accident.

Derived from the Latin word torquere, the root meaning of the word tort is twisted. Today, this root has taken on a new dimension. While tort still applies to victims with twisted limbs, it also aptly describes the contorted game of tort litigation.

When everyone agrees who is responsible for the incident, more serious and complicated questions come up. Was the incident the cause of the claimed injury? What is the extent of the injury? What is the economic loss? When these issues have been resolved, the most important question is encountered: what is fair compensation for the injury?

When the two parties involved cannot come to an agreement about equitable redress, they then call on the civil justice system for help.

We spend over $96 billion annually to provide that help, most of which is money down the drain. Of the million plus new lawsuits each year, over 90 percent are settled out of court. See Appendix, page 239. Only about two percent are submitted to juries. This is the first evidence of the problem. At least 85 percent of the lawsuits are nonproductive, proving to be of no value to either side.

By nonproductive, I mean the lawsuit doesn't benefit either party, the injured party, or the insurance company. The purpose of litigation is to help achieve justice. When the injured party is not offered an adequate settlement or any compensation at all, the only option is to litigate. If the claimant asks for more than a reasonable settlement, the insurance company is justified in allowing the claim to enter **litigation.**

Unfortunately, far too often the injured is offered fair compensation, but chooses instead to litigate. In some cases, the compensation is fair, but the insurance carrier refuses to pay, initiating expensive, time-consuming and needless litigation. Why this happens often is explained in this book.

Below are some typical examples, unfortunately, often encountered by the insurance carrier or by the injured.

BY THE INSURANCE CARRIER:

Muenzer v. State
Demand $100,000
Verdict $4,947,860

Rich v. Wilson
Demand $33,000
Verdict $900,000

Santilli v. Otis Elevator
Demand $17,000
Verdict $320,000

Scalia v. Sears
Demand $12,000
Verdict $150,000

King v. Safeway
Demand $5,000
Verdict $39,499

OR BY THE INJURED:

Huerta v. Josephs	
Offer	$500,000
Demand	$7,000,000
Verdict	$0

McElroy v. Firestone	
Offer	$1,000,000
Demand	$4,000,000
Verdict	$0

King v. Square D	
Offer	$125,000
Verdict	$25,000

Rodriguez v. City Of Visalia	
Offer	$65,000
Verdict	$11,500

Insurance Companies

Insurance companies spend about $45.7 billion a year defending personal injury claims. The most obvious costs are defense attorney fees, out-of-pocket costs and administrative costs which amounts to $17.7 billion a year. Adding to these direct costs, insurance companies often overpay claims to either avoid or to get out of litigation. This adds another $15 billion to their cost. It is not unusual for an insurance company to pay thousands more voluntarily than they anticipated paying at the hands of a jury. When the injury is serious, an additional five or ten thousand is not unusual.

More often, without checking to find out what a jury would likely award, often an offer that is already excessive may be substantially increased. Considering that we are dealing with millions of personal injury claims each year, with over a million cases, the overpayment can easily total $15 billion.

Less tangible items are increases in verdict size and payment of punitive damages and bad faith claims that tack on another $13 billion. Punitive damages and bad faith verdicts involving a claim of only a few thousand, can and often have exceeded a million dollars.

As is the norm with any industry, the cost of doing business is passed on to the customers. In this case, the policyholders absorb the costs through premium increases.

Policyholders

In addition to paying for the insurance industry's costs through increased premiums, policyholders who are sued have their own expenses.

Time spent with their attorney, in court and gathering information necessary for their defense quickly adds up, especially when the defendant is a business. The additional cost to someone sued for an automobile accident covered by his insurance policy can easily exceed $2,000. For the executive these additional costs can easily exceed $10,000. The months and years that defendants spend on litigation-related activities is worth $8 billion.

For large claims or those involving punitive damages, businesses may have to pay their own attorneys, or pay a part of the judgment. Businesses also lose sales or remove products from the market as a result of lawsuits or the bad publicity that often engulfs them.

Audi was sued for allegedly manufacturing an unsafe car that would allegedly accelerate on its own. Audi won the trial, but the unfavorable publicity caused them to lose a significant share of their United States market--with losses in the millions. While it is difficult to estimate the extent of lost business and other business costs, our $7 billion is realistic, yet conservative.

In the end, policyholders spend at least $60.7 billion on litigation annually.

The Injured Claimant

Litigation can be a very costly game for the injured. Some view the injured claimant as a hustler looking for an easy mark, when in fact the claimant is often a victim of litigation.

Because litigation takes years, the claimant is robbed of prompt compensation and often ends up with less money than if the lawsuit had been settled earlier, even for a smaller amount, due to inflation and expenses. While expenses and loss of personal time contribute to the loss, inflation and lost interest are larger factors.

With no early settlement to invest and earn interest, an injured person with the average automobile case can forego a couple thousand of dollars in potential interest income. For example, losing the interest on a $10,000 settlement for one year at 6 percent equals $600 in lost. With simple interest, the loss is $1,800 (for three years) and $5,400 (for nine years). Because inflation increases prices, it actually decreases the buying power of any money received after wading through the courts. If the claimant got $100 today, he could buy seven days worth of groceries. In three years, $100 would only purchase five days worth of food.

The expenses and losses add up to nearly $10 billion a year. The tragedy is that often the injured and the injured's attorney are unaware of the loss.

The Plaintiff Attorney

Many books and articles blame out of control litigation on attorneys who represent injured claimants. While some allegations are true, what is not realized (often by the attorneys themselves) is that litigation is costly to the plaintiff's counsel. Attorneys often take cases from which they could have made several thousand dollars an hour, work hard over many years and end up not even covering their overhead. Worse yet, their clients are penalized as well.

Many attorneys don't realize the immense capital and manhours required by today's litigation. For example, a single rear end collision back strain case, with a probable verdict value of $10,000 will take an estimated 80 hours through verdict. The litigation costs alone are $4,005. On a 1/3 contingent fee basis, the fee of $3,333 doesn't cover the out-of-pocket overhead costs. Not only will the attorney have nothing to show for the professional time involved, he will have to dig deep into his pockets for an additional $672! Yet, in 11 percent of the cases where the injured is awarded money, the verdicts run between $1 - $9,999. This does not take into account the 37 percent of the cases that jurors award nothing. Attorneys have large amounts of capital tied up in overhead, associates cost, secretarial costs and litigation expense. If they put that money in the bank, many attorneys' income would go up, and they wouldn't have to work.

Many attorneys concentrate their practice in representing the injured and have been doing so for years without realizing they may have several million dollars of their own funds tied up in pending cases. For example, $4 million invested at six percent could have yielded $240,000 annually. The attorney may often work long hours, including Saturdays and Sundays, and still net less than what he could have by investing the money tied up in the litigation.

Considering the loss of interest and the mounting expenses of litigation, plaintiff attorneys and their firms lose at least $7.5 billion a year litigating cases.

Self-Insurers

Because liability insurance is so costly and often not available, more and more entities are insuring themselves or retaining larger deductibles. These include businesses, non-profit institutions such as hospitals and to a very large extent, governments, including municipalities.

Insurance alternatives have grown consistently over the past couple decades and they now account for nearly 30 percent of the insurance, self-insurance market. Because traditional insurers spend $45.6 billion in litigation, we assume that self-insurers spend another $15 billion on the same items.

Actually, it is most likely much more. Insurance company claim departments are staffed by professionals. Often, self-insurers, especially local governments are not. Studies show that their cost of settling and processing personal injury claims is much greater than insurance company costs.

Taxpayers, Jurors and Employers

Aside from the increased premiums that taxpayers pay as insurance policyholders, they also maintain the court system. While it has other functions such as criminal cases, about $800 million a year goes to administer and judge personal injury cases.

Another estimated $200 million is paid, either by the courts or by employers, to jurors for their time and expenses while on jury duty.

The Total Estimated Annual Cost Of Litigation (In Billions)

Insurance companies defense fees, out-of-pocket costs, company supervision, overpayment	$46
Policyholders time spent in litigation-related activities	$15
Injured Claimants losses due to litigation delays	$9
Plaintiff Attorneys interest and expenses lost in litigation	$8
Self-Insurers defense fees, out-of-pocket costs, company supervision, overpayment	$17
Taxpayer civil court system	$1
TOTAL	$96

This is the cost for cases to proceed through the court system or the loss resulting from that process, not the compensation itself. There were an estimated 579,955 lawsuits filed in automobile cases in 1991 and the average payment is estimated at $25,113. Plaintiffs will be paid $15 billion. Another $26 billion will be paid to claimants in non-auto cases. Of the 509,505 lawsuits, the average payment was $50,688. **To deliver $41 billion dollars in compensation, $96 billion is spent or lost.** (We have not deducted plaintiff attorney fees from the $41 billion).

There is some overlap between these two. For example, insurance companies pay an extra $10 billion in compensation to get cases out of litigation, so that it is included in both estimates. They also pay $7 billion in compensation in bad faith and punitive damage claims. Eliminating this double counting, the cost to deliver the compensation is $79 billion. However, much of that $17 billion spent on overpayments, bad faith and punitive damages is unnecessary.

#4

The Opening Bet: Insurers Gamble 40 Percent Of Your Premiums

Plaintiffs and their attorneys are often pegged as the high rollers of litigation, risking everything for the chance of a big verdict. The insurance companies, however, risk as much. A jury orders a doctor and hospital to pay $2.6 million to the family of a dead patient. The doctor and the hospital turn to their insurance company. That is what insurance is for, to protect policyholders against monetary losses. Property and casualty insurance protects people who are responsible for damaging another's property or causing injury to someone. Life and health insurance protect people against expenses as a result of an illness or death.

"In a large part, because of insurance coverage, Americans: employees, business, home and car owners, have more financial protection, and security than any people anywhere have ever enjoyed in the history of the world," boasts the Insurance Information Fact Book.

This sense of security isn't cheap. The insurance industry had assets of more than $1.96 trillion dollars in 1990.

The property/casualty segment of the industry accounted for $556 billion of those assets. They collected $217.8 billion in premiums and employed some 623,300 people, according to the Fact Book.

Personal injury lines, one portion of the property/casualty segment, accounted for $97 billion of that premium total.

Automobile insurance accounts for about half of all of the personal injury insurance coverage. It is the largest coverage line that is having the most problems. Looking at all companies combined, auto insurance has not made a profit since 1980. In 1990, for each dollar that auto insurers earned, they spent that dollar plus 8.2 cents, which adds up to a $3.8 billion loss.

Other personal injury lines include commercial automobile, medical malpractice, homeowner multiple peril, of which about 40 percent is personal injury and the remainder is property coverage and other liability that includes a large amount of business coverage, including product liability coverage.

About 80 percent of all personal injury premiums are used to administer and pay claims, according to ratios reported by A.M. Best. About 25 percent are underwriting expenses or the cost of getting new business. Investment income makes up the difference, and when possible, provides for a profit.

Although, only a small portion of the claims paid by liability insurers actually reached the litigation stage, the ones that do reach this level can be very expensive. Based upon a Rand Corporation study, we estimated that in 1991, 610,147 auto and 535,923 non-auto personal injury claims were filed in court.

It takes so much time after the end of a year to get accurate figures, that the lag time often spans several years. For example, the National Center for State Courts recently issued its annual report for 1990.

Based upon the All-Industry Research Advisory Council, (AIRAC) 18.1 percent of all automobile claims enter litigation.

Based upon figures provided by the Insurance Service Office, (ISO) 25.7 percent of commercial claims enter the litigation stage.

The costs outlined in this chapter are detailed in the Appendix.

LITIGATION COSTS

Liability coverage requires the insurer to defend any claims made against the policyholder and pay within policy limits any settlements or judgments that result.

The insurer knows that litigation absorbs much of the premiums they collect. However, they don't realize how much, because many of the costs are hidden, or not easily ascertained. Many look at defense fees, attorney and out-of-pocket litigation when reporting litigation expenses. Another obvious cost, is claim administration. Insurance companies spend $1.7 billion in salaries and office overhead to handle personal injury claims. The actual cost is most likely larger than this conservative estimate.

Litigation is a complex social and legal process, and there are many hidden costs other than the obvious costs.

A major expense that claim officials are less than talkative about, but recognize exists, is the overpayment of claims to avoid a risky aspect of litigation. Overpayment to avoid having the claimant resort to lawsuits totals at least $5 billion. An additional estimated $10 billion is spent overpaying claims that have started down the litigation path to prevent further litigation costs.

Because litigation occurs over time, inflation affects how much the insurer actually has to pay. When a lawsuit is pending, inflation drives up the size of verdicts, which in turn drives up the size of settlements. Inflation costs the industry an estimated $6 billion more.

Punitive damages and bad faith payments tack on an extra $2 billion to the bill. Guaranty fund assessments tacks on another $.5 billion. The guarantee fund assessment is expected to be increased because of the many companies going belly-up. Claims filed without fact or legal basis often called nuisance or frivolous claims, cost an estimated $5 billion.

To determine the size of each of these individual costs, all available evidence and estimates are explored. Since current estimates are not always readily available, some have been updated or gathered from existing data. The sources and calculations presented in this chapter are detailed in Appendix A, page 240.

LEGAL DEFENSE FEES

Defense attorneys and expert witnesses may be the only two beneficiaries of litigation. The 1991 bill for defense fees in injury litigation, which include all direct litigation costs will be about $16 billion, according to data in the Insurance Services Office "ISO" report--Legal Defense: A Large and Growing Insurance Cost.

Defense costs, including attorney and expert witness fees, rose 320 percent between 1978 and 1988, according to the ISO report. The increase is much higher than the money paid to injured claimants, which only increased 190 percent during the same period. Defense fees are increasing in size, and as a percentage of payments. Defense fees were 9.6 percent of payments in 1978, but by 1988 they had grown to 13.9 percent.

Delayed litigation has been a significant factor in contributing to these skyrocketing defense costs. Numerous economic factors also can inflate the final cost of litigating a case. Expenses inflate due to time, requiring additional time of the attorney, because the case is pending. Interest that could have been earned and used for expenses is lost, because the money is tied up in litigation. For example, a case requiring $10,000 in defense costs is in the courts for nine years. The inflationary factors will balloon the final bill to $22,373.

Rand Corporation also studied legal defense costs in the 1985 report, Cost and Compensation Paid in Tort Litigation. Based on that report, costs and applicable growth rates, Rand's estimates put the 1991 cost of legal defense between $13.5 billion and $14.1 billion.

Because the ISO study is the most recent data, $16 billion is probably the most accurate estimate.

OPERATING EXPENSES

Like any other enterprise, insurance companies have basic operating costs that are necessary to conduct business. These costs, are unallocated loss adjustment expenses, include claim staff salaries and overhead expenses. Though they cannot be allocated to a specific claim, these costs still must be added in, because they are necessary to process lawsuits.

Estimates of the unallocated expense as a result of litigation from both the ISO and RAND put the total cost for 1991 at $1.7 billion.

Unlike defense costs, according to the ISO report, operating expense as a percentage of claim costs, has declined over the past decade. In the late 1940's, overhead settlement expenses were 18 percent of compensation costs. However, in 1987 and 1988, they accounted for only 9.9 percent of losses.

OVERPAYMENT TO AVOID LITIGATION

It is common knowledge among claims personnel, defense lawyers and lawyers representing the injured that the insurance companies will pay extra compensation to avoid litigation. Litigation costs money and may result in larger verdicts than expected. An insurance company that pays a little extra to avoid the cost of defense and the risk of a high verdict considers the extra payment worth it. This little extra, however, can be several thousand dollars; in a serious personal injury claim, it can easily approach $5,000 and sometimes much more. This extra amount may be increased several times in hopes of avoiding litigation.

The intimidation of a skilled plaintiff attorney can make litigation more risky for the insurer, especially in big cases with potentially large verdicts. When I was assigned to defend cases for insurance companies, if the home office supervisor didn't know the qualifications of the plaintiff's attorney, it was the first question he asked. Then and today, the reputation and skill of the plaintiff attorney affects the settlement amount. In a serious injury claim, this can be in the tens of thousands.

If the attorney is not a litigation specialist merely a general practitioner, the settlement offer may only be increased over the original offer by a modest amount. If that does not settle the claim, there may be another modest increase.

If the attorney specializes and is recognized as an effective plaintiff attorney, the increase is often more than if he were not. If that does not do the trick and the attorney threatens to file suit, another large increase may be offered.

The company's rationale is simple: "It is going to cost us money to defend the claim, so we will increase the offer by part, or half of our projected cost, to avoid the litigation costs". If that fails to settle the claim, the insurance company may increase the offer by the entire defense cost, on the theory that a verdict may run more than projected. The premium offered to avoid litigation can top the probable verdict plus the projected. The original offer may have been more than the probable verdict, yet it is still increased to avoid litigation. Unfortunately, the insurance company often fails to realize that the original offer is higher than the probable verdict.

An attorney's involvement in a claim, and the threat of a lawsuit, usually kicks up the payment. The average payment for automobile injuries in 1987 was $9,257 for attorney-represented claimants, versus $2,007 for claims that are settled directly with the claimant, according to the All-Industry Research Advisory Council reports entitled Compensation Paid in Automobile Injuries in the U.S.

The study showed that severe injury claims are more likely to end up with an attorney. This can account in part for the difference in payment. It is clear that much of that increase is also a result of overpayment to avoid litigation.

There is no way to use existing figures to estimate how much money is paid to avoid having a lawsuit filed. From my experience, however, and from watching settlements reported to Jury Verdict Research, a company which I owned, I would estimate that the figure exceeds $5 billion a year.

OVERPAYMENT TO GET OUT OF LITIGATION

Insurance personal and attorneys realize that companies will overpay claims after a lawsuit has been filed to get out of litigation. The rationale is the same: it is worth it to save the cost of defense and to avoid the chance of a high verdict. Often, the premium is on top of the extra money already offered by the company in an attempt to avoid litigation first place.

As attorney involvement and the threat of a lawsuit hikes the payment, so does the actual filing of the lawsuit. The ISO study Claim File Data Analysis--Part I, looked at claims worth more than $25,000 and found the average payment when a lawsuit was filed, was $93,918, in contrast with an average payment of $63,154 when no lawsuit was involved.

Part II examined claims of all sizes. When money was paid, the average payment was $37,099 with a lawsuit and only $5,893 when no lawsuit was involved. The following chart clearly shows the threat of a verdict brings nearly four times as much money as a verdict for the plaintiff. The increase can be large if the insurance company was recently floored by a verdict against their insured that was many times greater than expected. Some companies will almost frantically overpay to avoid trial.

Large verdicts against other companies frequently send shock waves to companies that simply read or heard about them. The shock translates into instructions to up the ante on those lawsuits with potential, to avoid trial, so there is no risk of losing.

Part II Closed Claims

Litigation stage	Average payment
No suit filed	$5,747*
Suit filed	
Settled before trial	35,871
Settled during trial	120,102
Plaintiff verdict	33,209
Average loss	16,384

*This table includes cases in which no payment was made.

The ominous nature of the courtroom can obviously result in gross overpayment. Look at the difference in the payments made during a trial. Look at the payments made before trial, and those payments with a plaintiff verdict. Knowing this, many attorneys representing the injured will make no serious effort to settle a case until they are in the trial room. Some believe they can extract the largest settlement by starting to impanel the jury.

Part of the reason for higher payments when lawsuits are involved, is that some lawsuits and trials involve serious injury cases. However, this does not account for all of the many differences nor does it account for the high payments made during trial.

There are no studies that indicate exactly how much money is spent overpaying claims in litigation based upon my cases as counsel for defense and plaintiff, and the observation of cases reported to Jury Verdict Research. From conversations with many personal injury attorneys and claim officials of insurance companies, I estimate that $10 billion a year is paid over the value of claims simply to get out of litigation.

INCREASED COSTS DUE TO ANNUAL GROWTH IN VERDICT SIZE

Burgeoning medical costs and inflation push the size of verdicts up every year. Since 1963, the average increase has been about eight percent annually, according to Current Award Trends by Jury Verdict Research Inc. The 1992 report showed an increase for 1990 of 7.67 percent. For 1991 (incomplete) it shows an increase of 8.12 percent. Insurance companies end up paying this increase if there is delay in making payment, whether its through settlement or verdict.

Commercial claims essentially those involving corporate defendants oftentimes are larger cases that spend more time in litigation. With these, the increase quickly mounts. The average two year delay costs the insurance company $8,621 per average claim or a total of $4.4 billion in 1991.

Automobile cases, however, are worth less and are resolved more quickly, minimizing the effect on that portion of claims. No insurance company will sneeze at the $1.6 billion absorbed by inflation on automobile claims.

Between auto claims and commercial claims, insurers pay an extra $6 billion, because of the delay and increased values inherent in litigation. Unfortunately, some insurance defense counsel and insurance companies consider any approach to inherent in litigation. Unfortunately, some insurance defense counsel and insurance companies consider any approach to settle as a sign of weakness. This is the reason that it is better to wait until the injured's lawyer approaches them. Many attorneys representing the injured feel the same way. The result is litigation needlessly pending and the insurance company paying more because of the increased values.

Complete calculations and sources are cited in the appendix. The following chart shows how the increasing verdict size is reflected in the insurance company's litigation costs.

<u>Increased Costs Due To Time In Litigation</u>

	Auto	Commercial
Average payment per case (1991)	$ 25,113	$ 50,668
Annual increase (verdict size--1989)	8.17%	8.17%
Average length of litigation	16 mo	24 mo
Average value increase (during litigation)	$ 2,812	$ 8,621
Number of cases	579,995	509,505
Total payment in average coverage	$ 1,630,945,940	$ 4,392,442,605

PUNITIVE DAMAGES

Theoretically, punitive damages are meant to punish the wrongdoer and discourage others from engaging in dangerous and threatening activities. Recently, it has also become a tactic to bump up the value of a claim. More and more attorneys representing seriously injured people are using this strategy.

In fact, the ISO studied the effect of punitive damages on the settlement of commercial claims. In claims of $25,000 or more, the study concluded that claimants who sought punitive damages got 60 percent more money: $133,445 versus $83,453. In a second study of commercial claims of all sizes, it was noted that claimants seeking punitive damages received settlements that were nearly 150 percent higher than claimants who did not: $37,000 versus $15,000.

The authors did note, "Much of the difference in claim settlement value between the claims with and without the threat of punitive damages may have resulted from the inherent characteristics of these claims rather than the threats". Nevertheless, as the respondents reported, punitive damage claims do have a strong effect on claim settlements.

Punitive damage verdicts can be frightening to an insurance carrier. The average verdict was $907,420 according to a 1987 study by Jury Verdict Research. More frightening, is that punitive verdicts can be gigantic.

Here are some factual situations that led to punitive damages. To illustrate the variety, the large verdicts and the importance of punitive damages, I cite eight cases.

A $9,000,000 verdict that included $8,000,000 in punitive

damages was awarded to a 40 year old female employee, who claimed to have suffered emotional distress when the defendant retail chain fired her and maliciously prosecuted her on the suspicion that she was attempting to shoplift. The plaintiff was detained while leaving work at the defendant store's premises and a search of her hand-carried hamper revealed $378 in unpaid merchandise. The plaintiff denied any knowledge of how the merchandise got in her hamper and volunteered to take a lie detector test. The plaintiff was acquitted of felony theft charges by an earlier jury.

A $10,000,000 verdict that included $8,000,000 in punitive damages was awarded to a 62 year old farmer. The farmer claimed he contracted polio from contact with his infant daughter who was given an oral polio vaccine. He contended the drug manufacturer was negligent by failing to warn of non-immunized adults contracting polio from contact with the drug. He also contended that the defendant was aware of the risk for ten years prior.

A $10,200,000 verdict that included $4,700,000 in punitive damages was awarded to an 18 year old female who suffered multiple injuries, including a brain stem injury that paralyzed the right side of her body, an injury to one of her vocal cords and decreased hearing in one ear. This happened after her vehicle was struck by the defendant driver head-on. The plaintiff also claimed the defendant driver was intoxicated. The defendant claimed to have had only two drinks, but refused a breathalizer test. Trial experts determined from police reports that the defendant driver had many more than two drinks.

A $5,001,000 verdict that included $2,350,000 in punitive damages was awarded to a 34 year old male roofer who suffered moderate brain damage. This resulted in loss of control of urges and irrational behavior after he fell and sustained a skull fracture.

The plaintiff went to the defendant hospital and was sent home by the defendant's doctor after X-rays were taken. The plaintiff contended the defendants did not notice the skull fracture. As a result, an abscess growth had formed. The defendants did not notice the abscess after the plaintiff returned to the hospital for a second time. The plaintiff contended the defendants were negligent and did not diagnose an obvious skull fracture. They did not call a neurological consultant or order a CAT scan. In addition to not having the patient admitted to a hospital, the defendants argued that they met the standard of care and that the damages were inevitable regardless of actions taken.

A $5,700,000 verdict that included $3,900,000 in punitive damages was awarded to the family of a 51 year old female homemaker. She was killed when her car was struck head-on by a delivery van that crossed the centerline. The decedent's plaintiff contended that the company that employed the driver was negligent for allowing the driver to drive on bald tires. The defendant company contended it did not own the van, and that it was not responsible for its condition. The decedent was not employed at the time of the accident but had planned to open a day-care center when her youngest child left for college. The decedent was survived by her husband and four adult children.

In the following cases, the punitive damage award for each was $8,000,000, which evidently is a prevalent figure with some juries.

A $13,000,000 verdict that included $8,000,000 in punitive damages, was awarded to a 61 year old male. The man was severely injured when a mobile home collapsed on him while he was trying to repair the undercarriage system. The plaintiff's lungs were crushed in the accident. The plaintiff contended that the mobile home was defectively designed and manufactured.

A $9,381,832 verdict that included $8,000,000 in punitive damages was awarded to a 15 year old female. The female was killed when her car, manufactured by the defendant motor company, was struck from behind and burst into flames. The defendant's vehicle's fuel tank was punctured by the rear axle in the collision and leaking gasoline ignited the fire. The decedent died 50 days after the accident of a broken cervical vertebra. She also had third degree burns over 40 percent of her body.

An $11,380,000 verdict, including $8,000,000 in punitive damages, was awarded to a 63 year old male rancher. The rancher suffered lung cancer when toxic chemicals spilled because of a train derailment and contaminated his property. The plaintiff was exposed to burning choloroprene, liquid formaldehyde and liquid monoethanolamine while trying to save his cattle and land from the chemicals.

As attorneys recognize the effect of punitive damages on

settlements, more lawsuits will be filed to seek them. The more common they become, the more worrisome and expensive they are for insurers and policyholders.

It's anyone's guess how much punitive damages cost insurance carriers. Their effect, however, must be significant since the serious injury cases always appear to specify an amount for punitive damages. I would estimate that the cost to insurance carriers now exceeds $5 billion a year. Punitive damages are growing rapidly and the figure will increase unless insurance carriers take effective steps to settle more claims without litigation.

BAD FAITH

In addition to protecting their policyholders against exposure to liability claims, insurance companies have their own liability exposure. **Bad Faith.**

The 1988 Jury Verdict Research, Inc. study, Bad Faith Actions Against Insurance Companies, analyzed verdicts in bad faith claims. It found that most claims fell into two primary categories: improper or inadequate settlement of a claim, and payment delayed or coverage denied.

Improper or Inadequate Settlements

More than half of the claims, 57 percent were for improper or inadequate settlement of a claim. They involved "allegations that an insurance company and/or the attorney for the insurer knew (or should have known) the equitable settlement value of a claim. And failed in their obligation to settle the claim for that amount", according to the study. Plaintiffs won 46 percent of these cases and verdicts ranged from $3,180 to $5,770,000. The median verdict was $102,375 and the average verdict was $808,280.

Payment Delayed

Plaintiffs in the second category payment delayed or coverage denied, won 72 percent of their claims, a much higher percentage than the first group achieved. Plaintiffs in this group "frequently charged that the insurance company, and/or the insurer's attorney, did not make or maintain timely payments of benefits". Verdicts in this category ranged from $1,445 to $10,150,000. The median verdict was $100,000 and the average verdict was $365,987.

When an insurance company cancels an insurance policy other than for a bad experience or a lack of cooperation with the insured, it may be considered bad faith.

An interesting segment of the JVR study is its analysis of punitive damages in bad faith verdicts. Of the plaintiff verdicts, 29 percent included punitive damage awards. Of those punitive awards, 40 percent were for improper or inadequate settlement, while 38 percent were for payment delayed or coverage denied.

One area of concern to insurance companies that ties into their bad faith exposure, concerns the insured's exposure to awards over the policy limits. When the insured is sued for an amount over the policy limit, especially with no independent counsel, failure to inform the insured of the probability of a verdict over policy limits, constitutes bad faith. The range of verdicts in similar cases is becoming costly to insurance carriers. This can be considered bad faith because informed consent was not obtained.

Lawsuits against insurance companies often include a combination of over-the-limit verdicts, inadequate settlement offers and delayed payments.

Since the JVR study referred to was made, juries have really taken insurance companies to the cleaners. For example: a $1,050,000 inadequate settlement verdict that included $675,000 in punitive damages, was awarded to an 11 year old male. The child was injured when the bicycle he was riding was struck by the defendant driver. The plaintiff's attorney settled the case for the $48,500 with the impression that the insurance coverage of the defendant was $50,000 rather than $100,000. The plaintiff contended that the insurance company of the defendant misrepresented the policy limits and acted in bad faith.

A $3,000,000 inadequate settlement verdict that included $1,500,000 in punitive damages, was awarded to a 27 year old female respiratory therapist. The therapist suffered multiple serious injuries in a vehicular collision with the defendant driver. The plaintiff contended she also suffered bad faith by the defendant insurance company for an inadequate settlement. The plaintiff also contended she was intentionally defrauded by the defendant's insurance adjuster.

An $8,002,000 verdict that included $5,500,000 in punitive damages, was awarded to an 18 year old male who suffered serious brain damage in an automobile accident with the defendant driver. The plaintiff brought suit against the defendant's insurance company for failure to come to a fair settlement. The plaintiff demanded the $100,000 policy limit. The insurance company representing the defendant offered only $60,000. The defendant driver joined the plaintiff in a suit against the insurance company for failure to pay the policy limit when the plaintiff's injuries warranted a settlement of more than the policy limits.

A $17,232,821 bad faith verdict (emotional distress) that included $15,000,000 in punitive damages, was awarded to the wife of a 29 year old medical technician. The woman was injured in a collision with a tractor-trailer. She charged the insurance carrier of the trucking company with failing to pay its policy limits, upon the opinion of its attorney, for the coverage in question.

A $20,130,000 verdict that included $15,000,000 in punitive damages, was awarded to a male nurse anesthetist. The nurse was the victim of bad faith by the defendant's insurance company, due to a conflict of interest. This occurred when the insurance company of the defendant refused to provide separate legal counsel to the plaintiff during a medical malpractice trial brought against the plaintiff and the hospital where he worked.

A $22,915,800 verdict that included $22,500,000 in punitive damages, was awarded to a 36 year old male, who claimed he suffered emotional distress when the insurance company of the defendant tried to implicate him in the burglary of his home. This was bad faith by a delay in payment based upon an unsubstantiated charge of misconduct.

A $57,000,000 bad faith verdict (inadequate settlement) that included $45,000,000 in punitive damages, was awarded to the surviving families of three adult male passengers killed in a plane crash. The decedent's families brought suit when the insurance company of the defendant did not make adequate settlement offers when the co-defendant was liable for producing an unsafe product. The insurance company of the defendant was a subsidiary of the co-defendant aircraft company.

Verdicts like these are important news to insurance carriers. They are often faxed immediately after being rendered to the insurance companies president's office. Most large verdicts like these can and do send severe chills to the carriers. The effect upon claim settlements is bound to be sizable.

The estimated cost of bad faith claims is more than $2 billion a year. Obviously, this will rapidly grow in size unless important steps are taken to prevent such litigation.

GUARANTY FUNDS

A new and looming cost for insurance companies is state guaranty funds. All states have or participate in automobile and casualty insurance guaranty funds when an insurance company becomes insolvent and can't pay its claims. The guaranty fund pays some or all the claims by assessing a portion of the cost to each of the state's remaining insurance companies. How much each insurance company must pay is based on its casualty/automobile premium volume in the state.

Since the number of insolvent casualty companies jumped from four in 1983 to 23 in 1989, insurers will be facing growing assessment. This is far below the 328 savings and loans that went out of business in 1989. The thought of another S&L debacle has focused a significant amount of attention on the stability of insurance companies, both property/casualty and life/health.

When premiums are cut by voter referendums or legislative action without considering root insurance company problems such as costs, the number of insolvencies can be expected to increase significantly. Rate rollbacks in California, Pennsylvania and other states can, and most likely will, result in more insolvencies and drain more money from the remaining companies.

Guaranty funds in states that refuse rate increases without solving the underlying problems also may be forced to increase the guaranty fund assessments. If these assessments become too large, which may happen, it will force additional insolvencies. The increased guaranty fund contributions, naturally, will find their way to increased premiums.

Not only are insurance carriers becoming increasingly insolvent, but more and more of them are large companies. The 1992 Insurance Information Fact Book reported, in 1989, insolvencies cost state guaranty funds $775 million. In 1990, the cost was $454 million, and over $3.3 billion over the years 1985 to 1990.

THE COST OF LITIGATION

The following table summarizes the annual cost of litigation for the casualty insurance industry.

ITEM	COST (in billions)
Defense fees	16.0
Unallocated loss adjustment expense	1.7
Overpayment to avoid litigation	5.0
Overpayment to get out of litigation	10.0
Inc. in verdict size/claim payment	6.0
Punitive damages	5.0
Bad faith claims	2.0
Guaranty funds	.5
Total Cost Of Litigation	$46.2

RESERVES

There are always people, including regulators and legislators, who think insurance companies hide large profits in reserves. Many do not understand, when a policyholder causes an injury that must be compensated, the money to cover the estimated cost of the claim must be placed in a reserve. Otherwise, when the claim is settled or tried to a verdict months or years later, the money to pay off the claimant may not be available.

Because the claims that end up in litigation are often the most severe, costly and takes a long time, reserves have become very large. Studies reveal, however, that many may be inadequate.

The Insurance Service Office did a Claim File Data Analysis study of closed commercial claims. The study showed a net under-reserved of $16 million or 26 percent of the claim values. Over a quarter of the claims (27.9 percent) were initially under-reserved by a total of $33 million. Claims were over-reserved by almost $17 million in 60.7 percent of the cases. About half of these claims were resolved without payment to the injured. When this happens, the money placed in reserves is taken down and becomes available to pay current claims. Likewise, when claims are settled for less than the reserve amount, the balance becomes available to pay current claims. When the payment exceeds the reserve amount, the balance is charged to current operations.

Of course, the money placed in reserve earns income. The value of the claims pending, however, increases faster than the income. Litigation costs further offset any reserve earnings.

#5

Policyholders May Never Play A Hand, But They Pick Up The Tab

Insurance policyholders bankroll the $46.2 billion insurers bet in the litigation game. They pump nearly $100 billion into insurance companies each year for liability insurance coverage and depend on the companies to bet it wisely. If their insurer makes some unsound investments, and needs more money to stay in the game, the policyholders bear the brunt by paying more for their coverage.

Drivers dominate the pool of policyholders in both numbers and dollars. There are 165 million drivers in the U.S., according to the National Safety Council, who collectively paid about $52 billion in insurance premiums in 1991. Twenty percent of these drivers have said paying their share of the insurance bill was a major problem, according to a 1990 survey by the Insurance Research Council. Another 40 percent said that paying for insurance was something of a problem.

After drivers, businesses bear the brunt of the remaining insurance bill. In 1991, $21 billion was paid in general liability coverage, which includes products liability, and coverage for accidents occurring on company property. Another $13 billion was spent to insure businesses' commercial vehicles.

Doctors and hospitals pay about $5 billion to traditional insurance companies and homeowners pay $8 billion, bringing the total to $98 billion. Insurance companies spend about forty-seven percent of that amount on litigation.

With all this money being pumped into the system, you would think the policyholders would be off the hook. No such luck, as defendants, they spend another $8 billion on litigation-related activities.

More far-reaching for the business community, litigation can kill products, break companies, and eliminate fairly priced insurance. It is difficult to put a price tag on these costs and losses, but I would estimate another $7 billion is clearly, conservative. If the business losses are not enough, all this comes with gut-wrenching uncertainty and anxiety.

It is clear, that litigation is costly to policyholders in many ways.

All cost estimates outlined in this chapter are detailed in the appendix, page 249.

ROUTINE LITIGATION COSTS

Once you are named in a lawsuit, litigation becomes a part of your life. It makes no difference whether you are the driver in a car accident, or the executive of a manufacturing firm.

Many lawsuits that are filed are a surprise to the insured and his carrier. For example, in products liability claims, the first notice of injury and product failure is typically the lawsuit. Nowadays, many manufacturers may contribute to the making of a single product. The lawsuit, thus, may be instituted against all of the companies involved.

In some states, attorneys often announce their representation with the filing of a lawsuit. Some lawsuits may occur many years after the initial use of or an exposure to a product. For example, in asbestos cases, medical problems that may have been caused by the exposure to asbestos may not manifest themselves until fifteen or more years later.

The litigation process starts with a court summons demanding compensation. This is followed by a trip to the defense attorney's office to sign the necessary legal papers and talk about the case. The claimant's lawyer usually orders a deposition of the defendant. Frequently, this necessitates a trip back to the attorney's office to prepare for the questioning. At the deposition, countless hours or even an entire day can be spent answering endless pointed questions.

A business executive in a products liability case may have to spend hours or days gathering information requested at the deposition (or by interrogatories), then return for more questioning. The interrogatories to be answered may consist of pages of detailed, written questions. It can take company officers and technical staff hours, days and even weeks to answer these interrogatories.

The defendant will then have to go to the pretrial, resulting in another day of lost work. There may be more than one pre-trial. If the case goes to trial, the defendant will be called in for a final preparation. That can last anywhere from hours to days. Next, the call to a trial room. For several reasons, after this final preparation, the case may be postponed or passed. This can happen before or after arriving at the courthouse. The next trial date may be so much later that the final preparation may have to be repeated.

Depending on the case, the court, the attorneys and the defendant may have to wait at the courthouse or their lawyer's office, sometimes for hours or days before the trial begins. The trial may take days, weeks or a month. Most defendants who have to take off work are not compensated for the time they miss and the lost earnings can be considerable.

While the loss for someone sued under an automobile policy may not be significant to some people, the 1991 average was $1,936 to $3,130 per case, which is still significant to the average policyholder. This totals $1.0 billion to $1.7 billion in defendant costs just for automobile litigation, according to updated Rand Corporation estimates.

When a company official or business is sued, particularly in a products liability case, it can cost tens of thousands of dollars. This amount also can exceed $100,000, to collect the data required by depositions and interrogatories, and to attend various legal processes.

A professional who is sued (particularly a doctor facing medical malpractice charges) can lose many thousands of dollars, especially when forced to forego seeing patients to attend court processes.

Costs for defendants in cases other than automobile, average $7,455 to $7,635 per case or an estimated $4.3 billion to $4.4 billion in 1991, according to updated Rand Corporation figures. With an increase in both the number and complexity of products liability and medical malpractice cases, and with the high cost for defendants to gather information, and the extensive loss of earnings, the actual cost is much more, at least another several billion.

Defendants spent at least $5.4 to $6.1 billion and probably as much as $8 billion on routine, litigation-related activities in 1991.

PUNITIVE DAMAGES AND POLICY LIMITS

The routine costs of depositions and trials can quickly be overshadowed by more serious problems, especially, if the defendant is named in a claim involving either punitive damages or over policy limits. In these cases, the defendant's role costs increase dramatically. The possible verdict can be very large. Combined with the uncertainty surrounding punitive damages, all steps to prevent such a verdict will be taken. This includes the use of expensive expert witnesses, and more discovery processes, which will increase the costs of defense.

Whether or not there should be a limit on the amount of punitive damages awarded in jury verdicts, is a hotly debated topic. The debates have reached as high as the U.S. Supreme Court. The two primary questions are whether punitive damages can be insured and whether they should be limited by law. Businesses and insurance companies are looking to the courts to limit the amount of punitive damages that a jury can award. The Supreme Court, however, recently ruled against punitive damage limits. The issue of whether punitive damages can be covered by insurance is still undecided. While most states (twenty-six, and the District Of Columbia), allow insurance coverage of punitive damages, eight states forbid it, and another eight do not allow coverage unless vicarious liability is involved, such as an employer sued for the acts of an employee. Punitive damages are insurable in two states, unless the conduct of the defendant is ruled intentional. In six states, no precedent has been set.

The growth of punitive damage claims in cases of negligence or strict liability is a frightening trend for policyholders. Whether or not the plaintiff wins, these claims are distressing and expensive. To read or be told about an $8 million or $12 million punitive damage verdict will frighten anyone that is being sued.

In states where insurance companies can't write policies to cover punitive damages, the policyholder is at direct risk. The reason these states do not allow insurance coverage to cover the risk is that punitive damages are considered a form of punishment. If the insurance company covered the cost, the rationale is that the company not the culprit would be the one punished by the award.

Lawyers who specialize in representing the injured have discovered that they can get much higher settlements if they claim punitive damages. As the previous chapter noted, payments for claims with punitive damages have been as much as one hundred fifty percent higher than payments for claims without punitive damages. This is one of the reasons these claims have been increasing so rapidly.

Defendants may have to hire and pay their own attorneys in lawsuits that ask for more than their insurance policy limits or uninsured punitive damage claims. While claims over policy limits are common in private automobile accidents, few policyholders secure their own counsel. However, when professionals or businesses are involved, the defendants usually find it advisable to consult their own attorneys. Understandably, the fees can become overwhelming. Since the stakes are high and expensive, skilled trial lawyers will be retained. The defense moves that they recommend will dramatically increase the costs to the defendant.

In addition to attorney's fees, it is not uncommon for the policyholder to contribute to the settlement in over-the-limit and punitive damage suits. This is necessary sometimes to settle the claim, even if the insurance company is not paying the policy limits. These contributions are oftentimes in the tens of thousands of dollars and sometimes much more.

The defendant may think that it is better to pay part of a settlement to get the case resolved, rather than risk being slapped with a punitive damage award from a jury. There are no guidelines for juries to follow when granting punitive damages. When the compensatory verdicts are only a few thousand dollars, claims for punitive damage, as you are already aware, are often in the millions.

One punitive damage award can wipe out a small business or create heavy losses for even very large corporations. A 1978 verdict against Ford Motor Company included a punitive damage award of $125 million. The case involved an automobile accident in which the gas tank of a Ford Pinto ruptured, causing flames to engulf the passenger compartment. The direct cause of the accident was a drunken driver who rear-ended the Pinto. A 13 year old boy who suffered burns over 90 percent of his body in the accident was awarded $2.8 million in compensatory damages.

Being on the receiving end of any lawsuit is very nerve-racking, and the anxiety is compounded when the risk of punitive damages is added.

The Board of Directors of a large company that I defended was so concerned about a lawsuit that included a claim for punitive damages they had the company's president flown to my city twice to meet with me. Though the company had a strong case, and was one of several defendants, the claim was clearly without merit. A strong defense eventually prevailed. Still there was a lot of anxiety about the claim, **primarily caused by the uninsured punitive damage claim.**

Motorists sued for amounts above and beyond their policy limit, also can suffer a lot of anxiety. This anxiety is usually caused by worrying over what might happen if a jury awards more than what the particular policy covers. Will I lose my home? Will I lose my privilege to drive?

LOSS OF AFFORDABLE INSURANCE COVERAGE

Even if punitive damages are not part of an automobile claim, the policyholder is often still punished because of being sued and is no longer able to get insurance at the preferred or regular rates. This forces the policyholder to pay the higher rates of a high-risk insurer. This can add over a thousand dollars to the insurance premiums.

Businesses involved in litigation may face skyrocketing premiums when they try to renew their policies. The insurer may drop the business. Then it has to shop around for insurance. Because it was dropped by a company as a result of litigation, other companies either may not want to insure it, or only want it at a much higher rate. For a medium sized company, the additional cost of insurance can easily amount to the tens of thousands of dollars. For a small company the amount added may be in the thousands of dollars.

Increasing liability premiums concern businesses even if they are not involved in litigation. In the 1987 Small Business Survey, published by Arthur Andersen & Company, nearly seventy-five percent of the executives queried reported liability premium increases greater than ten percent over the previous year. Another thirty-five percent paid increases greater than 25 percent in 1986.

"The justification of these increases to small businesses are not apparent since almost seventy-five percent of these companies had no increase in litigation when you base it on the number of actions, or the dollar amount of the claims. In spite of this, these companies had insurance premium increases comparable to those of companies with increased litigation", as reported by the Small Business Survey.

In the 1989 survey, 65 percent of the executives in the Cleveland, Ohio area said they were still concerned about the cost and coverage of liability insurance. Another twenty-three percent said they were somewhat concerned. Forty-one percent of the executives said they were concerned about litigation and lawsuits, more than any other issue.

DEATH OF PRODUCTS AND DESTRUCTION OF BUSINESSES

Lawsuits and the unfavorable publicity that surround them also can kill a product or destroy a business. The loss of one product can cost companies hundreds of thousands and even millions of dollars. Unwarranted litigation cost one well-known foreign automobile manufacturer (Audi) hundreds of millions in lost sales alone.

Products liability awards and high products liability insurance costs have sent chilling reverberations through the business community. New businesses claim that they are unable to develop new products, because of the cost of insurance and the risk of lawsuits. This far-reaching effect on American business has received endless coverage in the media.

In the 1989 issue of the ABA Journal, Franklin Nutter, President of the Alliance of American Insurers is quoted as saying, "The threat of liability is having a chilling impact on the innovation and development of products".

In 1991, insurance trade magazines showed concern over the issue. The March 11 issue of The National Underwriter explored the effect of liability on the development and marketing of childrens' toys. William MacMillan, Chief Operating Officer of the Juvenile Products Manufacturers Association was quoted as saying, "Innovative and safety-oriented products never make it to the market", due to liability insurance concerns.

TOTAL COST OF LITIGATION

Litigation costs policyholders an estimated $54.2 billion a year in premium increases and routine litigation costs. There are no studies that examine the cost of punitive damages, over-the-limit payments, independent attorney fees, higher premiums, and lost business. I believe these additional costs must total at least $7 billion, bringing the policyholder's cost of litigation to at least $61.2 billion a year.

While we have put a price tag of $7 billion on the indirect cost of litigation for American businesses, others have put direct and indirect costs as high $300 billion. This amount was given by author, Peter Huber, in his book Liability and has been widely quoted in the business press. It is based on premiums totalling $80 billion in 1989.

The Journal of the American Medical Association reported that doctors spend $3.50 in defensive tests for every $1 of insurance premiums to avoid litigation. Huber concluded if each policyholder does the same, this country will spend $280 billion trying to avoid litigation.

Huber's estimate is mentioned here as a point of information, but is not included in our calculations.

#6

Victim Again: The Injured Lose $9 Billion

Many feel the injured claimant is like a card shark, looking for a way to take someone for big bucks. In fact, very often the claimant is a victim of the litigation game.

The injured person is victimized primarily by the delay inherent in litigation. It robs him of prompt compensation for his injury and economic loss. It robs him of the interest that could have been earned on an early settlement, which can compound quickly. In addition, inflation keeps chipping away at the purchasing power of the money that is finally received. Too often, after years of litigation, the claimant ends up with less money than he would have received had he settled earlier. These time-related economic factors eat up nearly $6 billion of the plaintiffs' money.

This overshadows the $1.5 billion for the plaintiff's share of expert witnesses, travel and other out-of-pocket expenses needed to bring their cases to trial, as well as the $1.8 billion in personal expenses, primarily income lost because they have to attend court proceedings.

The injured is also victimized by a lack of information concerning the value of the injury claim. Reading and hearing about large verdicts oftentimes gives one the impression that his claim is worth more than it really is. The offer by the insurance adjuster, even if it is realistic, may be rejected if the plaintiff unknowingly believes that it is unfair.

Plaintiff's counsel may have given the false impression that the case was worth more than was realized, especially to be engaged to handle the case.

These inflated expectations cause the claimant to turn down early realistic offers, and even final offers years later. Even if a settlement is reached later for a sum more than what could be expected from a jury, the claimant may become bitter over the conduct of their attorney, the judge, defense counsel, the insurance company, and the whole justice system. The reason: not being properly and timely informed. The risk involved cannot be underestimated. If a case is submitted to a jury, judge or arbitrator, the plaintiff risks getting less than what was originally offered or, worse yet, nothing at all. Juries, as previously noted, send 38 to 40 percent of all plaintiffs away empty-handed. If the injured prevails in court, appellate decisions may take away or cut the award.

The claimant's expectations have been built up and they may feel they've been crushed by a steam roller. Their dreams and plans for the pot-of-gold at the end of the rainbow in effect turns into one big nightmare.

Considering these economic factors, the injured's share, after litigation, can wind up being much less than what it could have been without litigation.

The costs outlined in this chapter are detailed in the Appendix, page 250.

SETTLEMENTS CAN EARN INTEREST OVER TIME

If a plaintiff takes an early settlement and avoids litigation delay, that money can then be put in a bank to earn interest instead of waiting the many years it can take for a case to be resolved through the courts. With conservative investments, a plaintiff can make thousands of dollars on these investments.

In many instances, an injured person's health insurance or automobile insurance will pay medical bills. This leaves settlement money free for investing. If the injury is serious enough, it costs more than the health or auto insurance will cover. The recovery from the injury claim is often large enough to cover the bills and leave money for investment.

According to Rand Corporation, attorney's fees and litigation costs average 31 percent of recovery. In the average commercial claim, the plaintiff has $34,961 left after paying these costs. In the average automobile case, he has $17,327. The following chart shows the interest that can be earned on these sums if each was invested. Six percent was selected because over the long term, most conservative investments would yield this rate of return. Of course, the interest rates fluctuate from month-to-month and year-to-year.

INVESTMENT POTENTIAL

	Commercial Litigation		Automobile Litigation	
Year	Interest Earned	Total Value	Interest Earned	Total Value
Base	@ 6%	$ 34,961	@ 6%	$ 17,327
1 year	2,098	37,058	1,040	18,337
1.33 years			1,407	18,734
2 years	4,322	39,282	2,142	19,468
3 years	6,678	41,639	3,310	20,637
4 years	9,176	44,137	4,548	21,875
5 years	11,824	46,786	5,860	23,187
6 years	14,631	49,593	7,251	24,578
7 years	17,607	52,569	8,726	26,053
8 years	20,761	55,722	10,289	27,617
9 years	24,104	59,066	11,946	29,274

The average commercial claim takes almost two years to litigate, according to the ISO, therefore, $4,322 of potential interest is lost on each claim. At least $2.2 billion worth of interest was lost on the 509,505 cases resolved in 1991.

In 1985, Rand Corporation reported automobile plaintiffs spent an average of 16 months in litigation. During that 16 months, $1,407 in interest was lost. With an estimated 579,995 automobile cases in 1991, the total value of lost interest was $.8 billion.

While cases may conclude within a couple of years, it may take much longer. Commercial claims can easily take five years or more. An insurance trade association executive reported that many cases were still pending after 15 years on the docket. With the increase in criminal cases, especially drug related cases, delays have increased in the trial courts, even doubling in some jurisdictions.

TIME SPAN BETWEEN INCIDENT DATE AND TRIAL DATE BY CITY

	AVERAGE		MAXIMUM	
CITIES:	Year(s)	Month(s)	Year(s)	Month(s)
Baltimore, MD	2	11	7	3
San Antonio, TX	2	8	6	11
Bronx, NY	4	8	13	5
Chicago, IL	6	2	16	10
Cleveland, OH	3	3	12	5
Dallas, TX	3	6	7	3
Denver, CO	3	1	9	6
Atlanta, GA	3	4	7	9
Houston, TX	3	10	6	3
Minneapolis, MN	4	1	6	1
Seattle, WA	3	11	15	8
Los Angeles, CA	5	0	14	1
New York, NY	5	5	15	5
Palm Beach, FL	3	3	8	10
Philadelphia, PA	6	1	12	9
Queens, NY	5	0	10	9
San Diego, CA	4	1	10	9
San Francisco, CA	3	11	14	5
St. Louis, MO	3	11	8	1
Boston, MA	5	11	9	10
Detroit, MI	4	4	10	8

Using the most conservative estimates, plaintiffs lose $3 billion in interest because of litigation each year.

INFLATION DECREASES THE PURCHASING POWER OF MONEY OVER TIME

One constant fact is that every year the dollar purchases less. How much less depends on the rate of inflation and its effect on the price of goods and services. Although the current inflation rate is about four percent, in the past, it has been as high as ten percent. Since the inflation rate changes from year-to-year and sometimes month-to-month, no one knows exactly what the rate will be while a case is in litigation.

If inflation is five percent, an item that costs $1 today will cost $1.05 in a year. In essence, $1 in a year will only buy as much as 95¢ would buy today.

When a plaintiff has to wait years to receive his money, its purchasing power continues to decline. The following table shows how a six percent annual inflation rate will affect the recovery of the average plaintiff in commercial and automobile cases. Again, this is calculated on the plaintiff's share. Six percent has been selected because of the frequency of its occurrence over a period of years.

DECREASED PURCHASING POWER DUE TO INFLATION

	Commercial Litigation		Automobile Litigation	
Year	Inflation	Total Value	Inflation	Total Value
Base	@ 6%	$34,961	@ 6%	$ 17,327
1 year	2,097	32,864	1,040	16,287
1.33 years			1,366	15,961
2 years	4,068	30,893	2,017	15,310
3 years	5,921	29,040	2,936	14,392
4 years	7,663	27,298	3,799	13,528
5 years	9,300	25,661	4,611	12,176
6 years	10,839	24,122	5,374	11,953
7 years	12,286	22,675	6,091	11,236
8 years	13,646	21,315	6,765	10,562
9 years	14,924	20,037	7,399	9,928

If the injured party in a commercial claim waits seven years to get his $34,961, it will only buy as much as $22,675 would have bought before litigation.

Since these commercial claims average two years in litigation, $4,068 worth of purchasing power is lost on each claim. For the 509,505 claims expected in 1991, this totals $2.1 billion in lost purchasing power due to the insured 6 percent inflation.

In automobile claims, each plaintiff loses $1,366 in purchasing power during the 16 months they are involved in litigation. In 1991, 579,995 automobile plaintiffs lost an estimated $.8 billion in purchasing power due to litigation delays.

Added to the $2.1 billion lost by commercial plaintiffs, the total lost purchasing power is an estimated $2.9 billion.

LITIGATION COSTS

It is expensive to file, develop, present, and try a case. The plaintiff, by way of his counsel must pay filing fees. In addition, expert witnesses charge for consultation and testimony, and court reporters must be paid to attend and transcribe depositions. These out-of-pocket costs are often paid by the plaintiff's attorney if the case is handled on a contingency basis who is reimbursed only if a settlement or plaintiff verdict is reached. Some attorneys expect and get the plaintiff to advance money for out-of-pocket costs. None or only a small portion of these costs would be incurred, if the claim was settled without a lawsuit. Better, Earlier Settlements Through Economic Leverage, another book the author has written, cost accounts representative personal injury cases. It also projects the various costs of litigation, based on the value of the case.

Using data from that book, the following table estimates the out-of-pocket costs of the average commercial and automobile case.

The costs incurred before filing a lawsuit are not included, because they are not part of the litigation process; they would be incurred whether or not a lawsuit was filed.

OUT-OF-POCKET COSTS

Case type	Compensation	Out-of-pocket
Auto	$25,113	$2,774
Commercial	$50,668	$4,056
Average	$37,901	3,415

Since the above are the costs to litigate to a verdict, and most cases are settled before trial, it is obvious that most cases settle halfway between the filing of the lawsuit and a verdict. About half of these costs, or $2,000, is the overall average cost per case. For the cases resolved in 1991, the totals were $2.2 billion.

These out-of-pocket expenses usually come off the top of settlements and plaintiff verdicts, so the plaintiff and the attorney each pay a share. For example, if the total recovery is $30,000 and $3,000 in out-of-pocket expenses are paid off the top, the size of both the plaintiff's share and the attorney's fee are affected. However, if the attorney receives a thirty-three percent fee off the top, the plaintiff would have to pay all of the costs. If we assume out-of-pocket costs are taken off the top of the recovery, plaintiffs actually incur two-thirds of the total or $1.5 billion.

Litigation expenses are far more than just these out-of-pocket costs. These expenses are absorbed by the attorney in the form of salaries for associates and paralegals, and for the expenses of running the law firm.

PLAINTIFF PERSONAL EXPENSES

The plaintiff also has personal expenses above and beyond these litigation costs. Like the defendant, there are meetings with counsel and court proceedings, forcing the plaintiff to take time off work.

When updated to 1991, Rand Corporation figures indicate lost wages per non-auto case are $2,110 to $2,570, or a total of $1.1 to $1.3 billion. However, there is a strong indication that the personal costs are much higher in these commercial cases.

The value of time spent in automobile cases totals $478 to $.8 per case, or a total of $.3 billion to $.5 billion, according to updated Rand figures.

Personal expenses account for $1.4 to $1.8 billion of the total litigation bill.

TOTAL LITIGATION COSTS

Between lost value and actual expenses, litigation costs of injured plaintiffs total $9.2 billion.

ITEM	COST (Billion)
Lost interest	3.0
Lost purchasing power	2.9
Out-of-pocket expenses	2.5
Personal costs	9.2

In the next chapter, we will discover that the attorneys representing the injured often work harder only to cost themselves $9 billion.

#7

Raising the Bet. Plaintiff Attorneys Risk $7.5 Billion

In the litigation game, plaintiff attorneys are blamed for hunting down the mark and setting up the sting. They are pinned with seeking defendants with deep pockets, promoting litigation for their own financial gain, and contriving ways to allege negligence.

While some charges are true, what people don't realize, even the attorneys themselves, is that litigation is often a losing game for attorneys representing injured clients.

An attorney spends hundreds and even thousands of hours on a case and has to pay support staff and office overhead for each case. As litigation drags on, costs mount and in many cases attorneys could make several hundred dollars an hour by settling them early. Instead, they work hard over many years and barely cover their overhead.

Many simply don't realize the amount of capital and man-hours required by today's litigation. The support staff salaries and overhead alone total an estimated $3.3 billion annually. Plaintiff attorneys often are not reimbursed the estimated $2.2 billion spent on out-of-pocket expenses.

Attorneys also sabotage themselves by accepting and litigating cases with no merit. They expect that the insurer will offer a "nuisance settlement" to avoid further litigation costs, and they will come out ahead. Cost accounting shows that these cases rarely produce a decent hourly return, and the attorney often ends up losing money. Since more and more insurance companies have discovered that nuisance payments cause more such claims, they are being cut out by some companies.

There are plaintiff attorneys who have made a fortune representing the interests of injured clients. In the 1989 edition of Forbes magazine, a list of the best paid attorneys in America was published. Forbes concluded there were 137 plaintiff trial lawyers who made more than a million dollars in 1988. The largest group of plaintiff attorneys are members of the Association of Trial Lawyers of America. Its 1992 membership is over 60,000. Of these, 30,000 are in the tort law section (those that handle personal injury). About one-seventh of one percent are in the elite league of million-dollar earners.

While there are surely thousands of others who makes a decent living or more doing plaintiff work, there are also thousands of others who struggle to make their plaintiff practice work, always looking for the giant verdict that will propel them into the ranks of the millionaires. What they often don't realize is that using litigation for such purposes can break them before they strike it rich.

The costs outlined in this chapter are detailed in the Appendix, page 253.

LITIGATION COSTS

Many plaintiff attorneys fail to realize that litigation decreases their income. This happens because many attorneys don't keep time records and make little or no effort to cost account their cases. I am always surprised when gathering information on attorney costs, by the attorneys representing the injured who have no concept of the time and money they spend to litigate their cases. Most don't have enough information to determine their hourly overhead cost.

Yet, to maximize their incomes, it is crucial that attorneys know what they have invested in a case.

In much of today's litigation, a partner has associates and paralegals working with him. While they alleviate some work, they add to the costs. Top-notch trial lawyers, even on the associate level, can command salaries over $100,000 a year. Each hour that an associate puts into a case on the average, costs the law firm $48 just for the salary.

Each hour spent on a case also requires the use of space, utilities, support staff and equipment. Overhead expenses are currently about $45 per attorney hour and $23 per paralegal hour, according to one leading source.

Attorneys also advance filing fees, expert witness costs and court reporter fees. These out-of-pocket expenses are considerable; even a simple rear-end collision case can run $1,505.

As a result of these expenses, litigation can become a formidable investment.

The tables in Better, Earlier Settlements Through Economic Leverage estimate support staff time, overhead costs and out-of-pocket costs, based on the value of the claim. They are used to estimate the law firm investment for the average lawsuit. The law office partner's time is not included because his fee is whatever is left after paying expenses.

The following table takes the average compensation for plaintiffs in automobile ($25,113) and other ($50,668) litigation and charts these expenses. These do not include costs incurred before the lawsuit is filed, since they are not part of the litigation process.

PLAINTIFF ATTORNEY
LITIGATION COSTS FOR AVERAGE LAWSUIT

	Compensation	Time & Overhead	Out of Pocket
		(Does Not Include Partner)	
Auto	$ 25,113	$ 4,481	$ 2,774
Non-Auto	50,668	6,788	4,056
Average	37,900	5,630	3,415

The above are the costs to litigate a verdict. We estimate that the average case is settled about halfway between the filing of the lawsuit and the verdict. Thus, half of the costs are used, as the overall average for litigated cases.

Accordingly, we estimate $3,000 as the average in staff time and overhead costs. With 1,089,460 cases resolved through litigation in 1991, the total bill is $3.3 billion.

The average out-of-pocket cost is about $2,000 per case or a total of $2.2 billion. However, the plaintiff attorneys absorb about one-third of this or $.7 billion.

So plaintiff attorneys spend approximately $3.7 billion per year in litigation or $3,400 on each lawsuit.

COST OF PLAINTIFF PARTNER'S HOURS

These costs do not include the value of the partner's time, so we must consider this time to get an accurate picture of all of the costs involved in litigation.

Rand's research concluded that the average plaintiff paid 31 percent in attorney fees and legal costs. However, fees of less than 33 percent in litigated cases are uncommon. In fact, 40 percent is more prevalent. In some cases, especially the high risk cases, the fee can go as high as 50 percent.

Based on average compensation of $37,900, the average 31 percent contingency fee equals $11,749. Since attorneys spend about $3,400 on litigation costs, they net about $8,349 per case.

Assuming the partner handles about half of the work and delegates the rest, he will spend about 65 hours litigating a typical case to a verdict, according to Better, Earlier Settlements Through Economic Leverage. Since we assumed that the case will settle halfway through litigation, a partner spends 32.5 hours on the average case.

What is the partner's time worth? This will vary for different attorneys in different cities and in different specialties. The median billing rate for partners in this country is $150 per hour, according to Altman & Weil's 1990 Survey of Law Firm's Economics. Some command less than $100 an hour and many will command $200, $300 or $400 an hour. For illustrative purposes, we will use the nominal amount of $100 an hour that equals $3,250 per case.

For the 1,089,460 cases resolved in 1991, the time spent in litigation by law partners was worth $3.5 billion.

We have not considered the two percent of cases that go through litigation to a verdict or those that go into post-verdict procedure. We will not add for these, because we are making conservative estimates.

EFFECT OF TIME

Litigation often takes years, reaching five years or even a decade. As the plaintiff loses interest and purchasing power during the wait, so does the attorney.

The plaintiff attorney's share of an early settlement can be invested, where it can double in size. Instead, the plaintiff's lawyer receives nothing until after he wades through litigation.

Additionally, a plaintiff lawyer's firm that handles personal injury may, without realizing it, have several million dollars in total outstanding costs for its clients' cases. Many attorneys who are partners or sole practitioners may discover they would make more money not working than they do working if they just put that capital in the bank and lived on the interest.

Then there is inflation. Lawyers (three to five years after a lawsuit is filed) often congratulate themselves on getting thousands of dollars more than what was originally offered, not realizing that due to inflation he may have lost twice that amount in purchasing power alone.

TOTAL LEGAL FEES

Attorneys representing the injured earn between $13 and $15.7 billion a year in legal fees from litigated personal injury cases. How much of that do they pump back into the litigation system?...about half.

PLAINTIFF ATTORNEYS LITIGATION COSTS

ITEM	COST (IN BILLIONS)
Time and overhead costs	$ 3.3
Out-of-pocket costs	.7
One-third of $2.2 billion	
Value of partner time	3.5
TOTAL COST OF LITIGATION	$ 7.5

LEGAL MALPRACTICE

Aside from the cost considerations, plaintiff attorneys have the growing threat of malpractice to worry about. Many insurers are charging very high liability premiums for attorneys. The attorney pays for liability protection that, however, does not protect the attorney's reputation or practice when charged with malpractice by a dissatisfied client.

When attorneys litigate cases that end up paying nothing or less than the injured person was offered early in the process, a malpractice claim may result. Many attorneys don't realize that 37 percent of the cases tried to a verdict yield nothing and another 29 percent are for less than $50,000. This is a key point when an attorney considers how much it costs to litigate a case to verdict.

1990 DISTRIBUTION OF VERDICTS

Jury Verdict Research Inc.

Verdict Range			Percent of total
0			37%
$1	-	9,999	11%
10,000	-	49,999	18%
50,000	-	99,999	8%
100,000	-	199,999	7%
200,000	-	399,999	7%
400,000	-	799,999	6%
800,000	-	999,999	1%
1,000,000	+		5%

THE BOTTOM LINE - PLAINTIFF ATTORNEYS

Many attorneys handle cases with little merit either because of a lack of liability, shaky liability, or a questionable injury and enter them into litigation. If the insurance carrier refuses to pay nuisance settlements, or offers very little, the plaintiff's attorney then may be lucky to receive a small settlement or verdict or nothing at all. His share, if any, may not even cover his expenses.

Obviously, if the case is big enough, the plaintiff attorney will make money. However, it still may not be as profitable as settling, considering the massive investment required in litigation.

A look at a few of the individual cases cost accounted in Better, Earlier Settlements Through Economic Leverage sheds light on the time and costs involved in different cases.

The following table totals the associate and paralegal salaries, office overhead costs for the partner, associate and paralegal and the out-of-pocket costs for some representative cases. These are only the costs incurred between the filing of the lawsuit and the verdict or appeal. Costs before the lawsuit is filed are not included, because they would be incurred even if the claim had not been litigated.

TOTAL LITIGATION COSTS FOR SAMPLE CASES
PLAINTIFF ATTORNEY

	Verdict	Trial Costs	Post-Trial
Liability			
Rcar-end collision, lumbar strain	10,000	4,869	
Auto passenger, rib fracture	30,000	11,674	
Pedestrian accident, pelvic fracture	80,000	12,786	17,691
Defective ladder, fractures both legs	130,000	23,279	30,037
Falling elevator, multiples injuries	575,000	53,768	67,222
Industrial machine, leg amputation	1,750,000	56,881	71,625
Delayed diagnosis, wrongful death	1,100,000	79,774	89,647
Childbirth, brain damage	4,000,000	171,689	185,248

How does these expenses affect the partner's net return? More detailed cost-accounting of these cases examines at the plaintiff attorney's actual costs, and shows how quickly money is lost.

For example, take the $10,000 rear-end collision case. See the appendix, page 254. When the partner handles half of the litigation functions and gets a 33 percent contingent fee, a $1 an hour loss is incurred before a suit is filed. At pretrial, the loss goes up to $61 an hour and at trial it's $100 an hour. This is amazing, because 11 percent of all plaintiff verdicts are for less than $10,000.

Let's look at the cost of the case with a $80,000 verdict value. See the appendix, page 256. This example involves a pedestrian accident and pelvic fracture. If the partner performs 50 percent of the litigation functions, the net for the partner for settlement prior to suit would be a healthy $439 an hour. This, from a $33,451 settlement before filing suit is higher than if settlement comes at any point thereafter.

PARTNER YIELD OR LOSS PER HOUR: $80,000 VERDICT VALUE - PLAINTIFF ATTORNEY

$156 at pretrial
$34 during trial preparation
-$11 at the point of a verdict
$155 from plaintiff verdict
-$185 from a defense verdict
$90 successful appeal of a plaintiff's verdict

The hourly return is not only larger before the lawsuit, but if the $8,773 fee had been taken and invested, it would be worth $13,166 in five years, assuming a 6 percent return.

The time spent actually handling cases is what produces the money, but it is not the attorney's only job. Many attorneys overlook the fact that they spend many hours interviewing and investigating cases that lack merit and are not accepted.

Many cases that are accepted don't pay anything, but the attorney may not discover this until after expensive, time-consuming court processes. The hourly rate realized by productive cases must cover these costs that can be formidable.

Add to that the time required to run the office, attend required legal education courses, and the attorney is hard put to get in 1,200 productive hours in a year. Doing so, however, at $100 an hour would yield $120,000 in fees. After paying office overhead costs, which usually are one-third (frequently 40 to 50 percent) of income, the attorney will be lucky to net $80,000 before taxes.

#8

The High Rollers: Defense Attorneys Play A Loose Game

Defense attorneys may have the only sure bet in the litigation game. They defend the defendant and get paid, win, lose or draw.

However, this unpredictable climate is changing. Cost-cutting insurers and self-insured corporations are targeting defense bills. And they are trying everything from taking bids to building larger in-house litigation teams.

Many companies figure that by taking bids on routine or high-quantity litigation, they will get more competitive rates and smaller legal bills. Law firms may bid low in the hope that volume, complex cases, and low cost associates can add up to a reasonable economic return. There are reports that some law firms have concluded that they cannot make out on insurance company defense work and have withdrawn from such representation or are in the process of doing so.

Many companies that have a volume of litigation in one area can build an efficient and effective in-house litigation staff. This trend is burgeoning.

When insurance carriers don't have enough volume to hire in-house specialists or to work out competitive legal charges, they are beginning to hire law firms that can settle lawsuits promptly without overpaying.

It is clear, defense firms can no longer thrive on across-the-board litigation. Nonproductive, routine litigation is increasingly becoming a liability and not a source of reasonable profit.

The future for insurance defense lies in the handling of complex cases involving important liability or injury questions. When cases fall within a firm's expertise and strength, they can get the best results on a cost-effective basis. Even in the handling of these complex, important cases, insurance companies are conducting periodic audits and comparing costs to similar litigation handled by other firms. These measures may already be cutting into defense attorney salaries. While partners in defense firms still make more money than plaintiff trial lawyers, the gap is closing quickly. In 1986, defense attorneys made 21 percent more than plaintiff counsel, according to Altman & Weil's Survey Of Law Firm Economics. By 1989, that gap had closed to a mere four percent with the average defense partner earning $142,250, and the average plaintiff attorney's earning $137,000.

During that time, plaintiff attorney's income grew 40 percent while defense counsel income only grew 20 percent.

Whatever steps the industry takes to control costs, the defense bar has to respond to keep its clients happy. The emphasis in defense will continue to be in finding law firms that have the information and personnel to settle lawsuits promptly for fair amounts.

More insurers will find it to their advantage to pay a premium to those attorneys and law firms that can settle lawsuits promptly without overpaying them. Those who cannot will lose defense assignments. A growing requirement will be for law firms to accomplish settlements without expensive legal procedures such as depositions, pre-trials and trials.

#9

The Side Bet: Self-Insurers Ante Nearly $18 Billion

Tired of bankrolling the insurance companies, many policyholders have decided to play their own hand in the game. Doctors, hospitals, attorneys, government bodies, agencies and corporations are taking on the job of insuring themselves.

Self-insurance and other insurance alternatives for practical purposes started in the 1970's when liability premiums started climbing. When the situation worsened in the early 1980's and premiums skyrocketed, or insurance wasn't available, alternatives gained a major foothold in the insurance market.

Organizations with sizable assets and budgets, like big cities and major corporations, simply took on the job themselves. Many formed their own captive insurance companies. Others simply began performing insurance functions like setting aside the money to pay claims and hire attorneys. Smaller entities, like doctors and small cities pooled their funds. The pool provided their members with liability coverage.

Now, 28.1 percent of all property/casualty coverage is through self-insurance, captive insurance companies, risk retention groups and policyholder programs, according to a recent Johnson and Higgins study.

The people who really got slapped by the insurance crisis of the early 1980's have even higher rates of self-insurance. A 1988 survey by the Public Risk Management Society revealed that 79.5 percent of the public entities surveyed had some form of self-insurance. Over half of them reported that their general liability was covered through self-insurance or risk pools. The Insurance Information Institute estimates that 40 percent of all medical malpractice insurance is written through companies owned by doctors.

As with anything else, there are pros and cons in alternative insurance. The advantages outlined by the trade journal Business Insurance are that a self-fund "enjoys increased cash flow, does not pay premium taxes, does not contribute to insurance company profits, and is not subject to residual market and guaranty fund assessments". However, the editorial continued, "those savings can be wiped out by big losses stemming from ineffective loss prevention and loss control programs. Also from poor claims management, huge increases in the cost of medical care or a runaway liability judgment".

"No one knows if these groups are more or less effective handling claims and litigation than conventional insurance companies. Because the industry is so young, self-insurers and pools have not started databasing their information like conventional insurers," according to Professor John Pine, Louisiana State University.

An Insurance Services Office study of government and municipal injury claims did find that municipalities pay more for smaller claims and more of their claims end up in lawsuits than in general. For claims under $25,000, the average payment by a government defendant was $6,803 while the overall average was only $3,673. However, the average payment in claims over $25,000 was comparable. The majority of government claims involve lawsuits - 75 percent of small claims and 88 percent of the large claims -- compared with only 32 percent of all claims. One reason cited for this was the short statute of limitations on government claims. If claimants don't sue early in the process, it may be too late down the road, if negotiations aren't fruitful.

Based on the fact that conventional insurers spend $45.7 billion in litigation, we can assume that self-insurers spend another $17.9 billion on the same items: defense fees, claim supervision, to avoid or to get out of litigation, increases in verdict/settlement size, punitive damages and bad faith.

#10

Hoyles Rules: Billion Dollar Juries With The Final Say

With sweaty palms and a racing heart, the novice joins in the high-stakes game. But in this game, unlike many others, the novice has an important part: deciding who's got the winning hand and what it is worth. This privilege doesn't come free though. Taxpayers fork over $900 million for the site and jurors and their employers kick in another $100 million to man the jury box.

The calculations used in this chapter are detailed in the Appendix, page 258.

COURT COSTS

Some people fund litigation through insurance premiums, others through consumer prices. But every taxpayer pays to build and maintain courthouses and pay judges and their staff. They pay for tort cases, millions of other civil disputes like domestic relations, contracts and small claims, plus juvenile cases and criminal cases.

To resolve tort cases alone, a half a billion dollars was spent in 1985, according to Rand Corporation's Cost and Compensation in Tort Litigation. Updated to 1991, the total state and federal court expense is estimated at $862 million.

JURY COSTS

This is just a portion of what it actually costs to process a case through the system. Jurors must be called in and paid for each case that reaches trial. While it may seem like a minor issue, the cost of paying for jurors mounts quickly.

Since we know there were approximately 1,089,460 tort lawsuits concluded in 1991, and the National Center for State Courts (NCSC) reports that 2.94 percent of all tort lawsuits go to a jury trial, an estimated 32,030 jury trials were held in 1991.

Jury fees

To avoid overestimating the cost of juries, we will assume all tort jury trials are heard by eight person juries, even though 12 person juries are used in many instances.

The NCSC reported that most juries of eight people with two alternates were selected from panels of 22. Each person spent one day going through the selection process. The jurors and alternates spent an average of three days in trial. The eight jurors deliberated two days. This means each trial required 68 individual juror days.

In another report, the NCSC reported the average daily juror fee for each state. In 74 percent of the states, the local or state government pays the jurors and the average rate is $14 per day. In the remaining states, the losing party in a civil suit pays jury fees through the court costs. Fees paid by litigants are not added here since they were taken into account when we talked about the plaintiff's and defendant's costs.

With 32,030 jury trials using 68 days each and 74 percent of the states paying $14 a day, state and local governments' bill for jury fees is $22,564,495.

This is only the time each person actually spends on a specific tort case. In most counties, citizens spend a couple of weeks on jury duty, whether they are selected for a case or not. Adding the cost of these jurors-in-waiting would increase the total substantially.

Just to see how high the cost might be, assume that the 22 jurors called for each tort trial are serving a two week term. At $14 each, the bill would be $92.5 million.

Travel reimbursement

The same group of people who receive jury pay from state and local governments receive mileage reimbursement. The average rate is 14 cents a mile. While the average distance traveled by a juror is not known, if it is a 30 mile round-trip, $6,769,350 is spent in travel reimbursement.

As with daily jury pay, this estimate is obviously very low. Jurors who live in rural areas may have to travel 40, 50 or 60 miles a day to serve at the county seat. Even in major metropolitan areas, large segments of the population live farther than 15 miles from the courthouse. Plus, like the daily pay estimate, this only takes into account jurors involved in specific tort trials.

However, this estimate does provide some insight into how quickly a small item like 14 cents a mile can add up to a multi-million dollar bill.

Juror's lost income

Only six percent of the jurors in the NCSC study reported that they lost income during jury duty. At the average of $60 a day, jurors lost a total of $7,840,944 in income.

Unlike the two previous categories, this calculation is based on the total number of jury trial days, not only those paid for by the government.

Employers' cost

While the remaining 94 percent of jurors did not lose money, the employers who paid them lost productivity. With the average daily wage of a non-farm worker in the U.S. at $70, employers paid $112,822,430 in wages to absent employees.

This cost is for wages only, not the social security and benefit costs that employers pay for many of their workers. This calculation again only takes into account the jurors who go through the selection process or are selected to serve on a jury. There are many, maybe millions more who are called to jury duty, attend for two weeks, yet never actually serve on a jury.

Total cost to taxpayers, jurors and employers

Court administration	$ 862,336,501
Jury fees (paid by government)	$ 22,564,495
Travel reimbursement	$ 6,769,350
Jurors' lost income	$ 7,840,944
Employers' cost	$ 112,822,430
Total	$1,012,333,720

Next, Part II, where the kibitzers and players blame each other. In Chapter 11, we consider expensive trials and the clogged court dockets.

#11

Beefing Up The Pot: Expensive Trials And Clogged Court Dockets

Bluffing and stalling in a jam-packed casino. That's what litigation often resembles as attorneys and litigants maneuver their way through a congested, high-stakes court system.

EXPENSIVE TRIALS

Years ago, trials were much simpler and, in turn, much less expensive. A jury could be selected and deliver the verdict all in the same day. Serious injury cases took maybe three days and a five-day trial was quite unusual. Then Melvin Belli introduced demonstrative evidence, using charts, tables, pictures and experts to improve his client's chance of winning and of getting a large verdict.

What Belli started, attorneys for the injured have continued to refine, introducing more and more witnesses and exhibits to prove who was at fault, to prove their clients injuries and even to prove economic losses. Of course, defense attorneys have followed suit.

Now, one week trials are common. Some stretch into several weeks and even a month is not unusual. Just picking the jury in an important case can take hours or days. The court may even run out of prospective jurors during the selection process and have to adjourn to call a new group. In important cases, an expert may be called in to assist in the selection of the jury. In very important cases, a mock jury may be selected, hear condensed accounts of the evidence and then be interviewed by experts. This gives the attorneys and litigants an idea of what they can expect from a jury and helps them select the actual jury.

One way for attorneys to convince juries that their arguments are sound is to get an expert to back them up. More and more experts of all kinds are being used in court, especially in products liability and medical malpractice cases. This not only lengthens the trial, but increases the cost. Expert witnesses, especially leading experts in their field, charge hundreds of dollars an hour for consultations, reports and their appearance in court. Many experts are located across the state or across the country, so the lawyer must go to the witnesses' offices or bring the experts to their office for depositions. Either way, the time and transportation expenses add up quickly. When a witnesses' testimony is the key to the case, it must be transcribed by a court reporter, so the attorney can use it when questioning other witnesses and preparing for trial, adding more expense.

Exhibits, which have also become increasingly important in successful trial work, are another major expense. Exhibits range from anatomical drawings or models that help the attorney illustrate the nature of the injury to videotapes of a day in the life of the plaintiff, showing how the injury has resulted in a changed life style. They often require meetings with the supplier to outline what is needed. Working models are often necessary. A machine or tool may even have to be purchased. For example, in a product liability case involving the alleged malfunction of a factory machine, a similar machine may have to be bought for the investigation and for demonstration in court.

More sophisticated trial presentation isn't the only thing adding to the length and cost of trials. The law itself is continually getting more complicated, requiring more and more legal research. A whole team of people will often be involved in preparing an important case for trial. At the top will be the principal trial lawyer, assisted by one or more associate lawyers, who may be doing most of the work with the help of paralegals and law clerks from the law firm. They may need a nurse to interpret medical records and investigators to help get all of the information possible about the incident and the people involved. All of these people will work on developing the case and may even be required at the trial.

The length of today's trials spills over to increase the cost of appeals. With longer trials, naturally the trial transcripts becomes longer and more costly to reproduce. They must be analyzed by the appellate lawyers who then prepare briefs. With greater complications and length, the expenses follow suit.

Between the witnesses, exhibits, research and personnel, preparing and trying a case has become a major investment for both the plaintiff and defense teams.

These costs are compounded by the delay now inherent in the civil justice system and personal injury in particular. Just getting to the point of trial is a major undertaking, incurring actual trial expenses are just one of the costs of litigation.

THE BULGING OF THE COURT SYSTEM

Reliance upon the courts in the U.S. is nothing short of astounding. According to the 1990 annual report for the National Center for State Courts, (NCSC) more than 100 million new civil and criminal cases were filed in State Courts and over 280,000 were filed in U.S. District Courts. This is more than one lawsuit for each of the 88 million adults in this country. While the overall caseload in state courts grew only moderately between 1988 and 1989, 2.3 percent for civil cases and 4.7 percent for criminal cases, this is not necessarily true of each component. Over the past six years, felony case filings have grown steadily, nearly doubling in some states. Since these most serious criminal cases require extensive court time and personnel, they put an extra strain on the court system. The NCSC report indicates the overall number of criminal cases filed in 1984, will double by 1994, if recent trends continue.

On the other hand, the trend in tort is inconsistency. Tort filings have not exploded as some observers would have you believe, but there have been spurts of growth, primarily because of changes in state tort laws. The major push for tort reform between 1984 and 1986 prompted a 23.4 percent growth in tort filings. In many states, plaintiffs rushed to file their claims before restrictive laws went into effect. Then there was little change between 1986 and 1988. Another spurt of 7.6 percent occurred between 1988 and 1989. This inconsistency makes it difficult to predict or plan for long-term tort filings.

Whether it is steep or moderate, the courts simply cannot keep up with this growing caseload. According to the NCSC report, "A strong and disturbing pattern in 1989 trial court caseload statistics is low clearance rates. Many, perhaps most, courts are experiencing difficulty in keeping up with the inflow of new cases. The number of new cases filed in 1989 often substantially exceeded the number of cases that were disposed of by the court".

Since the number of criminal cases is growing and they have strict time limits which give them priority over civil cases, the civil cases which are pushed to the back burner are encountering delays that may stretch to more years of delay. This is compounded by a civil caseload that continues to grow despite an increased focus on alternative methods of resolution like arbitration and mediation.

General jurisdiction courts, the courts that handle the majority of personal injury cases, absorbed 27.6 million new cases in 1989. This is 2,979 new cases for each of the 9,250 judges. Most, if not all, of the general jurisdiction courts have individual docket systems in which the judges are responsible for the docket. With newspapers and State Supreme Court, Chief Justices are already looking over the shoulders of judges and publishing disposal rates and docket growth. Judges are already working harder than ever and there is little hope that they will be able to substantially increase the number of cases they handle. In fact, the strain is so great that more and more judges are burning out and resigning. With the growth in felony cases that take so long to try, many judges are no longer willing to cope.

In many, if not most, jurisdictions, the public mood against increased governmental expenditures prevents the addition of more judges to handle the increasing caseload.

The same problems facing trial courts today will surely make their way to appellate courts, as reported by the NCSC. "Rising civil and criminal caseloads create problems that ultimately will be transferred to the appellate courts. More cases add to the potential pool from which appeals are drawn and appellate courts will need to cope with the consequences of the trial court caseload growth recorded during 1989, as the cases filed in that year reach judgment".

DELAYS IN PERSONAL INJURY LAWSUITS

The overcrowded docket is not the only cause of delay in the courts, especially in personal injury cases. As personal injury trials have become more sophisticated, a new breed of "super lawyer" has evolved. These attorneys not only specialize in personal injury, but have become masters at using state-of-the-art trial techniques and witnesses to build their cases.

Many lawyers devote their entire practice to handling personal injury, others file lawsuits for all kinds of personal injury cases as part of a diversified practice, and others take on only routine cases. However, when litigation or trial becomes necessary, many will refer their important cases to a super personal injury trial lawyer. Super personal injury trial lawyers have developed in both plaintiff and defense specialties. In many firms, especially large defense firms, sub-specialties such as arbitration, medical malpractice and appellate work has become common.

Even though, there are hundreds of thousands of lawyers in the country, comparatively few try serious personal injury cases. In most areas, the very successful plaintiff and defense lawyers accumulate a sizable backlog of personal injury cases. Theoretically, a personal injury case could be tried within a year of filing in many jurisdictions. It is not unusual for cases to pend for years, while trial lawyers on both sides to arrange a mutually available trial date.

Added to this, are the heavy dockets judges face, the demand to give precedence to criminal cases, the inevitable illness of judges, attorneys, litigants and even vital witnesses.

The ISO survey of commercial liability claims looked at the experience of 24 insurance groups. It took an average of 37 months after the injury for the case to be resolved. Sixty-two percent of the time or 23 months was spent in the court system.

One large insurer, known for its efforts to dispose of personal injury cases without litigation and certainly without trial, reported that it had a significant number of cases throughout the country still pending nine years after they had been filed. An insurance trade association executive observed that it can even take a decade or more to resolve a disputed commercial injury claim.

In 1989, Jury Verdict Research, Inc. surveyed cases tried by juries around the country during the prior three years. It revealed that most personal injury cases took many years to reach verdict, the average time from the incident to the verdict was four years.

Examples of the delay to trial in several American cities:

Chicago One case was tried after only four months, the shortest time frame in the survey. Yet, it took another case 16 years and two months after the accident before a verdict was reached. On average, the wait for the jury's verdict was six years and two months.

The **Wall Street Journal** reported that in January, 1990, there were 67,778 civil suits more than five years old pending in the Cook County court system and that the current maximum wait was eight years.

Cleveland	One year and four months was the shortest time frame, while 12 years and five months was the longest wait. The average was three years and two months.
Detroit	The quickest a case reached conclusion was two years and the longest was ten years and eight months. The average wait was four years and four months.
New York	The shortest time from the date of injury to verdict was one year and three months, the longest was 15 years and five months. The average wait was five years and five months.
San Fran.	The earliest a case was concluded was six months after the injury, the second shortest litigation time in the survey. Another case did not conclude for 14 years and five months. The average time from the injury to verdict was three years and 11 months.
Seattle	The earliest that a court case was concluded was one year and one month after the injury. Yet in another case, 15 years and eight months elapsed between the injury and the jury verdict. Overall, the average wait for trial conclusion was three years and 11 months.

Post Verdict Activity

A verdict by a jury does not end all cases. The losing party can be expected to file various motions with the trial judge, such as a motion for judgment notwithstanding the verdict, a remittitur and a new trial. No figures are available, but from my experience and observations, I estimate that in at least a third of personal injury cases and perhaps even half, one or more post-trial motions will be filed.

Generally, a brief must be filed with a motion requiring legal research and an answer brief by the opposition's attorneys. Most of these motions will be argued orally in court. Since most motions revolve around what happened at the trial, portions of the record must be written up by the court reporter.

The result of these is that weeks, and more likely, months may pass before the legal procedures have been disposed of and the judge has ruled.

The next step is to file an appeal. In every state, a litigant is entitled to a review by an appellate panel of judges. The National Center For State Courts in its latest report issued in February 1992, reported that the volume of appeals reached a new high in 1990, 238,007 filed. We don't know how many of these involved personal injury cases. I would estimate that in almost every injury case involving a major injury, or a large verdict an appeal will be filed.

An appeal usually requires a transcript of the entire record. This takes time to prepare and is costly, especially for a major case requiring many days or weeks of trial. Preparing the legal brief for each side is another major undertaking. For example, in a negligent child birth case involving severe infant brain damage, it was estimated that the attorney representing the injured spent 120 hours and $2,500 in out-of-pocket expenses. Likewise, for the defense. Assuming the defense attorney only averaged $100 an hour (a modest estimate), the post-trial cost just for the defense attorneys would be $12,000!

Equally important, the additional time in litigation from the filing of an appeal to a decision may take months and a year or more.

This doesn't end all cases. In important cases, a further appeal by the losing side may be made. Since the right to review by the next layer of court, usually referred to as Supreme Court, is not guaranteed, the first step is to persuade the court that it is important that they review it. If granted, the brief on the merits must be filed. This may be followed by oral arguments. The time required can be a year or more and, of course, considerable legal and printing expenses are incurred.

Even this may not end important personal injury cases. Attempts may be made to get into the Federal Court system.

Many litigants, I am told, who have tried litigation as well as the alternatives of arbitration and mediation, recognize that the court system still achieves justice better than any alternatives offered. Certainly, trial attorneys who represent both injured and the defendant clients, who have publicly stated their position, agree that the jury system is best. The problem is not the court system itself, but the delay and the expense before a case is heard.

THE ADVERSE EFFECT OF DELAY

This kind of delay, whether it is two years or a dozen, has a direct effect on the bottom line of a case. Since cases may pend for years, court procedures and depositions occur over those years and expenses are hit by inflation. The time lapse also affects the money paid to the plaintiff and plaintiff's attorney.

While some of these factors were touched upon earlier, when talking about the individual cost items of each party, their cumulative effect is explored here.

There are six primary time-sensitive factors that affect the bottom line of litigation:

* the decrease in purchasing power due to inflation;
* the interest potential lost due to a delay in receiving compensation;
* the increase in the time required by the attorneys;
* the increase in litigation costs;
* the interest potential lost on expense outlays; and
* the annual increase in verdict amounts due to inflation.

Inflation decreases the purchasing power of money over time

Inflation decreases how much a dollar will purchase in the future. If the inflation rate is six percent and it takes four years for the plaintiff to get $50,000, it will only buy as much as $35,037 would buy today.

The cost to litigate a case increases over time

Whether paying expert witnesses or paying associate lawyers, every expense associated with litigation increases over time, simply because of inflation. These increases cut into the plaintiff's recovery, the attorney fees and add to the insurer's cost.

During each year that passes, the attorneys must spend additional time handling the case. Even if nothing is really happening and they are just waiting for the court trial time to roll around, they must stay in contact with their clients and keep tabs on the progress of the case. Many judges will schedule additional pre-trials in hopes of working out a settlement. Although, some settlements will occur, pre-trial costs can add hours or even a day of legal expenses.

Interest potential is lost on delayed recovery and expense outlays

Because an early settlement can be invested and earn interest over time, when the settlement is not made, that potential to earn interest is lost.

The same concept applies to money spent on litigation activities. If the money had not been spent on litigation, it could have been invested in an interest-bearing account.

The increase in verdict value

The size of verdicts is going up about 8.17 percent a year, which increases the amount of a verdict received in the future. This helps to offset some other factors that decrease the plaintiff and his attorney's recovery, but it increases the insurer's cost.

Cumulative effect on the injured

When all of these factors are considered, we can figure out the present value of money received at some future date and determine how much a settlement received today would grow over that same period of time.

Table 10-A calculates the future value using the bench mark values used by most economists - 30 year vs. bonds of $50,000 taking into account the interest which could be earned on the money. This is compared to the present value of $50,000 received in the future. Present value is a formula which takes into account the other economic factors, including decreased purchasing power; the interest lost on recovery and expense outlays; the increased litigation time and costs; and the annual increase in verdict value. Of course, both future and present values fluctuate. As a result, the values used in Table 10-A, may or may not reflect current values when this book is read. However, they illustrate the effect of time on settlements and verdicts. For more information on these calculations, see Better, Earlier Settlements Through Economic Leverage.

Table 10-A
Effect of time on $50,000

Year	Settlement future value 8.375%	Verdict present value -6.36%
Base	**$ 50,000**	**$50,000**
1	54,188	47,010
2	58,726	44,199
3	63,644	41,556
4	**68,974**	**39,071**
5	74,751	36,735
6	81,011	34,538
7	87,796	32,473
8	95,149	30,531
9	103,118	28,705

So if the injured person gets $50,000 from a settlement today and invests it, he will have $68,974 in four years. If the injured person goes through litigation and nets $50,000 after paying attorney fees, it would be the same as getting $39,071 today. A verdict twice as large as the settlement, will be approximately the same as the settlement after five years. This is illustrated in the next table. Many attorneys and their clients may jump with joy on being greeted with a verdict twice the size of the offer five years previous. They don't realize that they gained nothing for that long court wait!

Table 10-B
$50,000 Settlement Compared to a $100,000 Verdict

Year	Settlement future value 8.375%	Verdict present value 6.36%
Base	**$ 50,000**	**$100,000**
1	54,188	94,020
2	58,726	88,398
3	63,644	83,112
4	68,974	78,142
5	**74,751**	**73,470**
6	81,011	69,076
7	87,796	64,946
8	95,149	61,062
9	103,118	57,411

The effect on the plaintiff's attorney is similar, but more pronounced. Because of the extra expense of paying staff members and expenditures for office space, the value of the attorney's share would shrink even faster than the plaintiff's share.

Obviously, litigation is both expensive and time-consuming for the plaintiff team.

The cumulative effect on the insurance carrier

How does delay affect the insurance carrier? For illustrative purposes, let's say if the case goes into litigation and is resolved within the year, it costs the insurance carrier $100,000 to defend the case and pay the plaintiff. The following table shows how much that bill will go up each year the case pends, due to the above cited influences.

The only thing the insurer has working for it is earnings on claim reserves. When a claim is made, the insurer puts aside money to pay it. Until the claim is paid or dismissed, interest is earned on that money. Unfortunately, for insurance companies and policyholders across the country, inflation and expenses offset their earnings on their claim reserves. In fact, after taking into consideration earnings on reserves, the average cost to insurers is 11.72 percent per year, according to calculations in Better, Earlier Settlements Through Economic Leverage.

Table 10-C
Insurer's cost

Year	Cost
Base	$100,000
1	111,630
2	124,613
3	139,105
4	155,283
5	173,342
6	193,502
7	216,006
8	241,128
9	269,171

(Annual increase 11.72%)

In just a couple years, 25 percent is added to the insurers cost and by seven years, its bill has more than doubled.

On the other hand, if the insurer had paid the plaintiff $50,000 before plaintiff hired an attorney and filed suit, that would have been its only cost. And as table 10-A shows, the plaintiff would still come out ahead.

#12

The Scam: 85 Percent Are Losing Hands

With millions of people gambling billions of dollars, you would expect many winners. However, in the litigation game, only about 15 percent are winners. The remaining 85 percent are losing hands.

Litigation only serves one purpose. If it benefits one of the parties, it is so expensive that the benefit must be significant, otherwise it is of no real value. It is clear that most litigation does not benefit either side, instead, it hurts them.

Measuring whether litigation is productive or not depends upon who's involved as well as its timeliness. For the person injured, prompt, adequate compensation for his injury is the main concern. An insurance carrier or defendant has to measure the overall situation and must consider whether the payment of a claim will encourage similar claims. If litigation prevents similar claims, then it is productive.

The plaintiff attorney whose trial skills and results are far superior to the opposition's may be entitled to a premium in the settlement amount over that of a less skilled attorney. Also, a noted defense attorney may call for a discount in the settlement amount. If these benefits cannot be gained through a settlement, litigation may be worth it. Considering every perspective, economics is still the driving force.

Unfortunately, most attorneys representing the injured rarely consider the importance of the bottom-line. **Very few attorneys have ever cost accounted their litigation. They overlook their own overhead costs, associates' salaries, and**

out-of-pocket expenses. They also overlook the injured's costs. Too many attorneys representing the injured forget the importance of earning interest on invested money. They also overlook a constant in today's economy, the erosion of buying power due to inflation.

Although tragic for them, it can be even more tragic for their injured clients. In trying to get more money for their clients, the injured claimants are deprived of prompt payment. Too often, after years of waiting they receive a settlement or verdict that is worth less in buying power than what they could have obtained without litigation.

Insurance companies often overlook some of their costs. Few consider that as cases pend, jurors often award more money. Unfortunately, for the injured and their attorneys, even when the verdicts reflect this increase, the increased costs and loss of interest often outweigh the increased value. Further, a settlement after years of litigation may not even reflect the increased value.

As a trial lawyer, and as President of Jury Verdict Research, I have observed the offers, the demands, and the results of many cases. I submit that at least 50 percent of personal injury litigation is non-productive and that the injured and his attorney lose money. Further, the defendant's expenses are compounded, whether covered by insurance or self-insured. In another 35 percent personal injury, litigation does not help materially. Thus, in 85 percent of the cases litigation did not serve any significant purpose. Needless litigation is detrimental to both the injured and the insurance carrier.

What happens to cases that enter litigation.

Let's examine some facts. Three recent studies show that approximately 90 percent of cases filed in court are settled before going to a jury for a verdict.

The ISO Claim File Data Analysis revealed that 91.8 percent of the commercial claims studied were settled before a verdict and 8.2 percent were tried to a verdict. AIRAC's, Compensation for Automobile Injuries in the U.S., revealed that 93.9 percent of automobile accident cases were settled before trial. And 2.8 percent settled during trial, while 3.3 percent were resolved by a jury trial.

The National Center for State Courts gathered data from several states that indicated only 2.8 percent of all tort lawsuits were resolved through a jury trial.

You can conclude that if over 90 percent of cases that enter litigation are resolved without being submitted to a jury, most likely there is no sound reason for most of them to have ever gone into litigation.

Of the cases that are heard by a jury, many result in verdict amounts that fail to cover the cost of litigation. The 1991 edition of Current Liability Trends, published by Jury Verdict Research, reported that in 1989, plaintiffs lost 37 percent of their cases heard by juries and received nothing. Over the years, 40 percent received nothing. Another 11 percent received less than $10,000 and another ten percent received between $10,000 and $50,000. Even receiving $50,000 a few years after the injury may not provide adequate benefit to the plaintiff after legal expenses, attorney fees, and medical expenses are paid.

Does litigation serve any purpose? The answer is yes.

Obviously, not all litigation can or should be eliminated. Litigation is vital in the resolution of tort claims, it simply has to be used more judiciously. In the purest sense, litigation helps maintain justice by making the negligent pay for whatever harm their negligence causes.

Litigation is necessary to help the litigants acquire the information necessary to settle cases and to resolve questions of injury, liability, value and law. It is not practical to use litigation to decide all disputes. Litigation is neither effective nor efficient for that purpose. It is especially effective for setting a legal precedent and in establishing the value of claims so later cases can be settled by following the verdicts and the guidelines set by the courts.

The first group of cases requiring litigation. For them to be properly evaluated and presented, requires information that can only be obtained through the court processes. In some cases, the injured person cannot prepare a case proving fault until key people have been deposed, including parties to the accident, witnesses and technical people. Similar depositions may be necessary for the defendant. It also may be necessary to take depositions to discover any prior injuries, the cause and extent of the injuries claimed, and/or the amount of medical expenses and lost income.

I estimate that no more than ten percent of the lawsuits currently filed need information that can be obtained only through the deposition process. However, once the information has been obtained, usually within a matter of a few months after the filing, most of these cases should settle.

Often the filing of a lawsuit would not be necessary if the parties cooperated with one another, without either side, the plaintiff or the defendant, compromising his position. The attorney for the injured could obtain most, if not all of the information he needed, without a lawsuit if the defendant and the insurance company cooperated. Also, the insurance company or defense counsel could get all necessary information without a lawsuit being filed. With this kind of cooperation, less than five percent of the cases would have to be filed to obtain essential information.

The second group of cases that requires litigation is those with serious questions of fault, injury, insurance coverage or law. More than just needing information, these cases involve irreconcilable disputes over the facts of the case. It could be unclear whether the injured person is entitled to compensation under the current laws. A court may have to interpret the laws for cases involving unique, ambiguous or emerging changes in the law. This often applies when an insurance carrier or company is facing many similar claims that involve the same product or incident. The facts of the accident also may be under dispute. For example, in an intersection collision with no witnesses and both parties claiming to have had the green light, litigation will probably be necessary to settle the dispute. Questions arise as to whether the injury claimed was caused by the accident, or if the injury is as serious as claimed.

I estimate that another ten percent of lawsuits filed need court processes to decide serious disputes about liability and/or injury questions. Although these important questions may require a jury trial to settle, as a practical matter, even most of these are resolved by compromise.

This means an estimated 20 percent of the cases that are filed require some court process and could be productive. Once the necessary information is obtained, which is usually (or should be) early in the process, some cases can be quickly settled, reducing the time and the cost of litigation. Unfortunately, once in litigation, most of these cases remain in litigation until they have become non-productive. This reduces productive cases by an estimated five percent.

Considering that some of this litigation could be brief, only about 15 percent of the litigation now in process is productive. The remaining cases (85 percent) are either harmful to the litigants, provides no benefit, or drag on beyond their usefulness.

What is productive litigation?

If an injured person is offered less money than is merited under the law, and fair compensation is obtained over and above the costs of litigation, then litigation is productive. Also, when an injured person or his attorney demands more than what is merited under the law, litigating to prevent this from happening also can be productive if the litigation is cost-effective.

If you use these standards to measure the extent of prudent and necessary litigation, only about 20 percent of the cases filed can be considered productive. Of these, less than 15 percent are productive once the necessary information has been obtained, and the litigation continues.

Of the cases submitted to a jury, a large portion should never have gone that far, because the insurance company had offered more money or the plaintiff demanded less money than the jury eventually awarded.

A study of final offers by Jury Verdict Research showed that 28 percent were larger than the verdicts. Of these, 10.7 percent were two to six times greater. In most of these cases, the statistical information available would have shown the plaintiff attorney that these offers should have been taken.

Similarly, 37 percent of final demands were less than the verdicts, many by hundreds of thousands of dollars.

Only 17 percent of the final offers, and a similar percentage of the final demands fell within the range of an acceptable valuation. That is 25 percent higher and 25 percent lower than the verdicts. Nevertheless, these were tried. Over 50 percent of the cases never would have gone to a jury if the lawyers had done their homework and discovered that jury trials were unnecessary in these cases. The results of this study reflect on the abilities of the lawyers and the insurance claim executives to determine the value and outcome of the case and are addressed in further detail in Chapter 14.

If non-productive litigation were eliminated, the same percentage of cases would still find their way to a jury. Since this accounts for about three percent of the total, and the total pending could be reduced by 85 percent, it would be only a minimal number of cases, thus, unclogging the court system. The result would be the end of the long delay to the court room.

The buttom line

Considering the high cost of litigation and the valid uses of litigation, 85 percent of it is nonproductive. It is nonproductive because it costs more than it returns.

Observation of the cases that have been submitted to juries reveals that only a small percentage involve serious questions of fact, or law. The greatest reason for submission to a jury is disagreement on how much the case is worth. There are less expensive ways to determine how much a case is worth, which will be explored in this book.

If 85 percent of litigation is non-productive, a like portion of the costs or $82 billion is being wasted in nonproductive litigation.

#13

The Politics. Casting Aspersions. Each Player Overlooks His Bad Play

In recent years, there have been hundreds of speeches, articles, books and even advertisements placing the blame for high insurance premiums. Each author has a favorite culprit, and the list is long. In laying blame, many people overlook important facts and draw widespread conclusions from few statistics. Those directly involved in the negligence compensation system often overlook their own role in the problem, but are quick to indict others. Interestingly, everyone overlooks the real problems, and workable solutions can only be formulated when the true causes are addressed. Before examining the real causes of non-productive litigation, it is important to take an analytical look at the various claims of blame.

Juries are out-of-control

The most popular culprit is the jury. Juries are often accused of being overly generous with insurance company money. Yet, they are responsible for a only small portion of the money paid to claimants and their decisions are generally conservative.

Of the lawsuits filed, about 20 percent of all personal injury claims, juries decide about three percent. Approximately 90 percent of all personal injury lawsuits are settled before they reach trial, let alone a jury. Of the cases that make it to juries, 37 to 40 percent of the injured people receive nothing and many are awarded relatively small sums.

1989 DISTRIBUTION OF VERDICTS

Verdict Range		Percent of Verdicts
	0	37%
$ 1	$ 9,999	11%
10,000	49,999	18%
50,000	99,999	8%
100,000	199,999	7%
200,000	399,999	7%
400,000	799,999	6%
800,000	999,999	1%
1,000,000	over	5%

Many of the large verdicts are eventually taken away, trimmed substantially or settled for a fraction of the original award. The Rand Corporation study, Post-trial Adjustments to Jury Awards showed that the ultimate payout on verdicts of $1 million to $10 million averaged 68 percent of the original award. Verdicts over $10 million, the ultimate payout averaged 57 percent of the original award.

Even if all of the verdicts delivered in 1989 were paid in full, they would amount to less than $4 billion. Considering our previous appraisal of litigation costs, it is clear that this is a minor portion of the total expense.

Further examination of large verdicts, excluding punitive damages reveals that in most of these cases the injuries and economic losses are very substantial. When the injuries, disabilities and economic losses are examined, I believe few reasonable-minded people would quarrel with the verdicts. Interestingly, of the large verdicts, many include punitive damages with some based upon the defendant's conduct in the handling of the claim. Unfortunately, brief accounts in the newspapers of all kinds of cases tried often give the impression that juries are awarding huge sums for minor injuries.

In some cases, the jury verdict is too high. In others it is too low, but we have legal mechanisms for dealing with these problems. The defendants, when claiming that verdicts are too high due to prejudicial error and/or passion and prejudice, they too often rely only on legal points of claimed error. They often overlook the corroborating fact that the verdicts did not fall within the probability range, which they could show by citing probability figures as well as actual verdicts. When a verdict does not fall within the probability range, it means that something happened at the trial that made it fall outside. The reasonable explanation is that the claimed error occurred. When defendants neglect to use such corroborating evidence, and the trial or appellate court fails to correct the verdicts, the defense counsel failed to do their job. Under these circumstances, defendants do not have a license to complain about what they consider an unjust result from the system. Those who blame runaway juries clearly are not aware of the 37 percent of all plaintiffs who receive nothing or the 29 percent who get less than $50,000. It is evident that they are people who read newspaper accounts of very large verdicts and have the impression that juries regularly pass out huge awards.

Jury awards are generally conservative when compared to demands by attorneys and payments by insurance companies for similar injury cases. The problem is clearly not juries, but the lack of information about jury awards by many who decide on settlement payments, especially on behalf of insurers and self-insurers. Those who blame juries without knowing or even considering the facts also contribute to this myth.

The liability system is unpredictable

Some critics claim that the unpredictability of our liability system is the problem. They are not aware that jury decisions are as predictable as life expectancy. No one can predict exactly how long any single individual will live, but we do know from clustering how long we can expect a person to live. Insurance companies can and do issue life insurance based upon probability, as to life expectancy. Likewise, good business decisions can be made for verdicts based upon probability. Unfortunately, many insurance companies rely on "the partially educated guess", which studies show is grossly unreliable. They don't bother to use verdict probability tables that have proven to be valid during over 30 years of continuous use.

"Insurance companies are ripping off the public"

Many people claim that insurance companies are making unconscionable sums of money and that they are hiding the money in reserves. The fact is, from 1969 to 1980, this country averaged four insurance company insolvencies per year. In 1989, there were 44 insolvencies and both the number and size of insolvent companies are growing.

Most insurance companies have never faced so many losses. Private passenger automobile insurance, which accounts for about half of all liability insurance, has been operating at a loss every year since 1981. For every dollar earned, insurers of private passenger automobiles have spent an average of $1.07. This takes into account premiums earned, investment income, claim payments, all operating and underwriting expenses. Insurers of commercial automobiles, which as we already mentioned, account for another 21 percent of the market have spent $1.06 for every premium dollar.

In the states that regulate premiums, especially in the automobile market, insurance is essentially a cost-plus operation. Insurers file requests showing their costs and asking for a reasonable profit. When the insurance commissioners do not grant appropriate increases or do just the opposite and roll back premium rates, insurers in such states have a problem even existing.

In the less regulated or unregulated states, the insurance rates are lower because the companies can compete freely. The problem is not the insurance companies ripping off the public but the stifling regulations.

"We have become a highly litigious society"

"The number of personal injury cases thrown into litigation is increasing dramatically".

However, the facts do not support this. Tort litigation is growing, but only slightly faster than the population. In 1985, Rand reported that the population growth between 1980 and 1981 was .95 percent. The growth in tort filing during that same period was 3.9 percent. In its 1990 annual report, The National Center for State Courts concluded, "Growth in tort filings between 1986 and 1989 was essentially flat, with as many states experiencing year to year decreases as increases". The National Center reported that there was just over a three percent increase between 1989 and 1990 of tort filings, but that all civil filings grew by over five percent. "The most dramatic increases in the civil caseload tend to be real property and contract cases, not torts".

The Director of the Court Statistics Project, Brian Ostrom, in a letter to me dated April 14, 1992, noted "the distinguishing feature of tort case filings is their susceptibility to short-term adjustments in response to changes in state statutes governing tort litigation" (usually preceding a change in tort laws).

"Claim-conscious lawyers are encouraging lawsuits through contingent fees"

Actually, a lawyer who is handling personal injury on a contingent fee basis is less likely to take a case of no merit. Lawyers who specialize in the handling of personal injury will knowingly take only those cases that they expect to be profitable. Unfortunately, because many are poor businessmen and have very little concept of the cost to handle cases, they book cases that they would not have taken, had they known the cost facts. But contingent fees do permit many injured people with little financial resources to present meritorious claims which they could not have pursued otherwise.

The problem is not contingent fees but uninformed lawyers who, without realizing it, take contingent fee cases that decrease their income and are of little or no assistance to the injured. When they discover the adverse economics, we believe these lawyers will be more careful in their selection of cases.

"The public has become claims conscious"

"Injured people want to be paid large sums for their injuries even if they were at fault", many cry. This is human nature and such desires have existed for generations. There is some truth to this, but under the law, the insurance companies need not pay non-meritorious claims. Unfortunately, many insurance companies pay, claiming that they are saving money. Often, all they do is encourage more litigation and cost themselves more in the end.

Unfortunately, many insurance companies pay the injured much more than a jury would probably have awarded because they think the jury would have awarded even more.

"Legislators and judges are creating liability situations where none existed before"

This has been occurring for many decades as modern technology has grown. The strength of our negotiation-jury compensation system is that it changes to meet new needs. The no-fault and compensation systems which some propose are inflexible and would either result in injustices or likewise would have to change as costs and other relevant factors changed. Where a new product causes injuries, the cost of compensating those injured by the product must be factored into the price. If a product cannot compete in the marketplace, it cannot be justified by exempting it from liability. Otherwise, what would those injured by it do?

The claim that the present liability system prevents products from being marketed is only true for those that have less utility than the cost of resultant injuries. Thinking people recognize that new products cannot be produced, especially complicated ones or new drugs without causing some injuries. This is why product liability insurance has been invented. It spreads the risk, but the risk is there and must be considered.

While expanding liability results in increased claim costs, insurance companies that are given timely notice can increase their premiums to cope. Of course, this results in increased premiums to policyholders. Is the increase in liability socially desirable? Is the public willing to pay the increased cost? These are question which must be answered before this practice is challenged.

"The present negligence system does not work; it is too costly and delivers little"

It is true that the negligence system is costly, but it does not need to be. Actually, no other proposed system can deliver justice as well as our present system. It is flexible and meets new needs. Some people are uncomfortable with change, but most can meet the changes necessary for a changing society. Injustice results when changes are not gradual.

The fault compensation system is a far superior system to

the compensation system along the lines of no-fault and industrial compensation.

These alternative systems rely on rigid schedules. They not only become out-of-date due to inflation and other changes, but they do not adequately compensate the seriously injured. Allowing lawsuits for the serious injury only, raises the cost, as unnecessary treatment to qualify is encouraged.

The claim is that they save money over the present system. This is true only where compensation schedules are unrealistically low.

#14

Playing Without The Hole Card: The Partially Educated Guess Dominates The Negotiating Charade

Settlement negotiations conjures up images of high-powered attorneys and slick insurance adjusters, backed by reams of documentation and convincing evidence, battling it out in glass and chrome conference rooms. In reality, it is more like a couple of back-room gamblers playing a hand of stud poker without bothering to look at their hole card.

Gamblers who play this way can expect to lose big and that is what many insurance companies and attorneys are doing. By operating in a jury system but being blind to what jurors do, they embark on an expensive self-defeating charade that they call negotiations.

The negotiators realize the role of juries and it is accepted that juries are the key in resolving personal injury claims. Professors Harry Kalven and Hans Zeisel of the University of Chicago School of Law, conducted one of the most comprehensive studies of American juries, observed:

"At every stage of this informal process of pre-trial dispositions, decisions are in part formed by expectations of what the jury will do. Thus, the jury is not controlling the immediate case before it, but the host of cases not before it which are destined to be disposed of by the pre-trial process. The jury controls not only the formal resolution of controversies, but also the informal resolution of cases that never reach the trial stage."

Everyone who negotiates, settles and tries personal injury claims talk in terms of what a jury would do with the claim since juries set liability and price. Few bother to find out what a jury would actually do. Instead, they rely on hearsay and their own limited experience with verdicts.

The injured read about large verdicts and expect the same

Large verdicts in any given locality are rare, and when they do occur they make local news. They may also receive important national media coverage in the newspapers, television and radio. This national attention gives the impression that large verdicts happen frequently in this country, even though they do not. As outlined in the last chapter, juries are generally conservative.

Equally important, editing to conserve space and make the story more interesting often distorts the facts, so it appears that juries are awarding immense sums of money for nominal injuries in situations that no one in his right mind would expect. When a defense verdict or even a small verdict occurs, it is not reported as news, except maybe in small local publications.

According to a recent survey commissioned by the Defense Research Institute, all the parties involved in litigation agree that, "the media promotes plaintiff side victories over that of the defense side ". More than 90 percent of the defense attorneys, 55 percent of the plaintiff attorneys and insurance executives polled recently, agreed with that statement.

Reading and hearing about huge verdicts for what appear to be minor injuries and no liability, no one can blame an injured person, especially someone who is seriously injured, for dreaming that their ship has come in; dreaming that after the settlement or verdict they will be able to retire in luxury.

Attorneys and insurance company personnel rely upon the partially educated guess

While reliance on limited knowledge can be expected from the injured public, this should not be true of the professionals in the system, yet it happens frequently.

Few attorneys have actual jury trial experience or bother to read verified reports or documented information about personal injury verdicts. Their information is often confined to what they read in newspapers (generally about large verdicts) and scuttlebutt around the office, courthouse or coffee shop about verdicts and settlements. Yet, everyone who handles personal injury claims talk in terms of what they expect a jury to do in a particular case.

Like the story of the blind men and the elephant, each person's expectation of the end result may be vastly different from the others. Why is this? Because there are so many variables involved in personal injury. In many instances, the case or some factor about the case may appear to be unique. Actually, most of the facts involved, other than the names of the litigants are not unique. The problem is that there are so many different liability and injury situations. Few attorneys and insurance personnel have sufficient knowledge to draw reliable conclusions of probable outcomes without consulting in depth the jury information that is available.

Over a million personal injury lawsuits are filed each year. Fewer than three percent of the personal injury lawsuits filed are submitted to juries.

This translates into approximately 32,000 cases decided by juries in a year. An estimated 350,000 attorneys handle personal injury cases. This is fewer than one case for every ten attorneys. About 20,000 attorneys primarily defend personal injury cases on behalf of the defendants. The Association of Trial Lawyers of America has about 50,000 members who primarily represent injured victims. Statistically, each of these specializing lawyers could be involved in less than one case decided by a jury each year. Actually, a handful of attorneys in any locality try almost all of the cases, especially the larger ones. Even a busy trial lawyer who does nothing but try personal injury cases may only have two or three cases go to a verdict in a year. A rare few might have ten or more, provided that none or only a few are important cases.

In the United States, there are nearly 900 insurance groups which write the majority of personal injury coverage. Although, a group may consist of several insurance companies with different names, essentially they function as one company. When you look at the number of insurance companies and number of cases tried by juries each year, it indicates that the average trial experience of any one carrier is very small. An average of 36 cases a year. Some companies try more cases than others, but still not enough to make valid predictions of jury reactions.

Some insurance companies specialize in certain kinds of coverage and will see more litigation in that field. For instance, State Farm Insurance Companies cover an estimated 20 percent of the nation's automobiles. They will see many automobile cases. Other insurance giants like Nationwide and

Allstate may also litigate more cases of this kind. Smaller companies have much less litigation exposure, simply because of their size.

The complexity of today's cases also affects the number of cases tried by one attorney or insurance company in any one category. Trial preparation takes a tremendous amount of time. Many cases settle in the courtroom without ever going to verdict. Even an attorney actively engaged in the trial of personal injury cases has personal experience with only a small number of verdicts. Serious injury or complicated cases may take weeks or even months to try. As a result, even a lawyer who works long hours has difficulty trying more than a handful of cases to a verdict in a year.

Another point to consider is that a case tried several years ago may not be a valid indicator of the value of a case today. As medical costs and wage losses increase each year, most verdicts also increase. Medical discoveries can minimize the consequences of some injuries or reveal that other injuries are more serious or of longer duration than previously thought. Technological advancement can change the outlook of a claim dramatically over time.

The different ways in which people are injured are endless. There are many different kinds of automobile accidents: rear-end collisions, collisions with objects, intersection accidents, turning collisions and many more. The Personal Injury Valuation Handbooks, published by Jury Verdict Research, study 22 different types of automobile accidents with 108 subcategories. Each products liability case may be different, because the number of products and ways people are injured are almost endless. There is medical malpractice, legal malpractice, engineering malpractice, premises liability and industrial accidents which all require intricate, specialized knowledge.

For example, if someone is injured in an aircraft accident, it requires specialized knowledge to determine what a jury would be expected to award. Information about how planes fly and how they are constructed is necessary. Knowledge of engineering problems and airplane equipment standards is also necessary.

If someone is injured by a machine at work and claims that the safety equipment failed, specialized knowledge of the construction and operation of that piece of equipment may be required.

Today's personal injury cases can be so technical and vary so much from state to state that few people can figure out what really happened and whose at fault. Let alone what a jury will be likely to do with such information.

The different types of injuries and their consequences are also abundant. Injuries caused by drugs or by the environment may be very different from more common bruises and broken bones. Oftentimes, such injuries do not emerge or are not recognized until years after exposure to a drug or environmental toxin. Also, injuries occur that were never seen before.

Any statistician will tell you that no one attorney, insurance company or insurance supervisor sees enough cases decided by a jury to be able to draw any valid conclusions. The hundreds of different causes of accidents, injuries, degrees of injury and economic loss which can be involved makes this impossible. Even if one attorney participated in the trial of all the cases in California in a year, the 1,610 verdicts would not provide enough statistically meaningful information to evaluate the different types of cases and injuries that the adjuster or attorney may encounter in California or anywhere else.

For example, a $10,000 verdict for a back strain case with $2,000 in medical costs and lost earnings would tell the attorney nothing about the value of a claim that involved the death of an executive earning $500,000 a year due to an alleged failure to diagnose cancer.

How does this limited experience affect negotiations? It creates the partially educated guess, evaluation and negotiation based on limited empirical data and extensive gut feeling. In turn, reliance on the partially educated guess makes attempts at settlement less effective because negotiators don't have solid evidence to back up their offers and demands.

Insurers negotiate with the claimants

With the doctors' reports, medical bills and evidence of lost income in hand, the adjuster approaches the injured person to settle the claim. This is probably the injured person's first claim. Nervous and leery feelings are running rampant. The only idea of what to expect is from newspaper headlines about large verdicts and attorney commercials that question the fairness of insurance company offers. As a result, the adjuster's first offer may be very disappointing. It may be far less than what had been expected.

When the claimant questions the offer, or rejects it, what does the adjuster do? The adjuster assures the claimant that the offer is fair. Like the poker player, a trusting smile is flashed. The message to the claimant is not one of trust.

Even though the offer may be fair, or may be more than what would be expected from a jury, does the adjuster offer any evidence of that? Is it shown to the injured person why the offer should be accepted? Is it pointed out what a jury would probably award? Are any odds given on the chances the injured person has of losing?

Is any data produced about how long it will take to get to trial? Is the claimant told of interest that would be lost during the many years of waiting? With few exceptions the answer is no. The adjuster keeps this pivotal hole card face down.

Although, the adjuster or insurance company has access to information that would convince the claimant that the initial offer is a good one, this information is usually never revealed to the claimant. In Settled Out of Court: The Social Process of Insurance Claims Adjustments (Aldine Publishing, 1980), H. Lawrence Ross found that jury verdict reports, routinely consulted by attorneys, "were seldom used by (insurance company) claims men".

What does the adjuster do instead? To avoid having an attorney brought into the case, the adjuster will probably hike the offer. This happens even when the initial offer is fair or even high when compared to the probable jury award.

Without adding evidence that the offer is fair, do insurance companies really expect adjusters to work out prompt settlements without the claimant running to an attorney? If they do, they are ignoring the facts.

A recent study by an insurance industry research group, the All-Industry Research Advisory Counsel, reported that attorneys represented 31.3 percent of all automobile claimants in 1977. By 1987, the rate was up to 44.6 percent. In serious claims (with economic loss over $5,000), 80 percent of the injured victims hired attorneys. The rate goes up to a whopping 98.5 percent in commercial claims when the payout is expected to be more than $25,000, according to the Insurance Services Office.

Insurance companies don't seem to realize that people today are both better educated and more skeptical. They will not simply accept an adjuster's empty statement that the offer is fair. They want proof. When no proof is offered, the injured is nudged into hiring an attorney.

The policy of simply increasing the offer is often counterproductive and may even contribute to an attorney being brought into the claim. After one or two increases, the claimant naturally thinks that all one has to do is refuse the offer and hire an attorney and the ante will keep going up.

Having driven the seriously injured to seek the help of an attorney, the game takes on a new twist, as both negotiators bluff their way into litigation.

The insurer faces the plaintiff attorney

The first round of negotiations between an adjuster and the attorney is that it allows each to scope out the other's tactics, skills and confidence level. It sets the stage for the negotiating charade.

Unless they agree upon who was at fault and the nature of the injury, settlement negotiations may not be pursued. However, in the majority of cases, minor disagreement over injury, fault, prognosis, medical expenses and lost wages are taken care of early in negotiations. The discussion centers on the settlement figure.

Attorney: "What is the insurance company prepared to

pay?"

Adjuster: "I don't bid against myself. What do you want?"

Attorney: "$500,000"

Adjuster: "You're kidding!"

Attorney: "No, I'm serious."

Adjuster: "What do you really want?"

Attorney: "My client is seriously injured. She has a sizable amount of lost wages and medical expenses. Her ability to work and to enjoy life is substantially impaired. She lives with a great deal of pain and suffering. You have all the medical reports and expenses. I think I'm reasonable in only asking for $500,000."

Adjuster: "With such an unrealistic demand, I can't even make an offer."

This may end it for now. However, both parties need to know where they stand, so some prodding may bring about further discussions.

Adjuster: "I'll pay $75,000."

Attorney: "You're kidding!"

Adjuster: "I'm just as serious as you are".

Are these two professionals talking about the same case? With the offer a mere 15 percent of the demand and a $425,000 difference between the two, clearly one or both of these negotiators are off track.

Attorneys' knowledge of personal injury case value is as

varied as the attorneys themselves. There are hundreds of different legal specialties, anti-trust, divorce, criminal, business, retirement, etc. which have no exposure to personal injury. Yet, most of the 700,000 plus attorneys in the country will book a personal injury case, especially a serious one that may involve a substantial fee. Even if unable to handle the case, the attorney will expect a portion of the fee for the referral. If the attorney cannot handle the case, the counsel will refer it to a friend who handles the occasional personal injury case or to a firm that specializes. The vast majority of cases end up with attorneys who handle only the occasional case.

The adjuster should be aware when dealing with a attorney who doesn't know the value of the case, and should use all methods of persuasion to show the attorney that the offer is sound. Yet, what does the adjuster do? Does the adjuster offer the attorney information on the probable verdict size, the chance of prevailing, the length and cost of litigation and the economics of lost interest and inflation? No, again he probably offers more money. Being an educated person, the attorney is not going to accept the word of the adjuster without evidence that the offer should be accepted.

So the case is pushed further along to litigation. Now, the insurer may bring in the big guns, the defense attorney, who picks up the game where the adjuster left off.

This game may seem unreal, but it is not a tale of fiction. In the book, Legal Negotiation and Settlement, Professor Gerald R. Williams of Brigham Young University wanted to judge the negotiating skill of attorneys and compare their results on the same case. He got 40 practicing attorneys from Des Moines, Iowa to participate in his experiment. They were randomly divided into 20 pairs, with one attorney representing the plaintiff and the other representing the defendant. Each attorney was given identical case files as well as copies of comparable jury awards from the Des Moines area.

The outcome of this experiment showed a dramatic difference in the attorneys' treatment of the case. Initial demands ranged from a low of $32,000 to a high of $675,000, while opening offers started at $3,000 and went up to $50,000. Of the 20 pairs, only ten arrived at a settlement. Four did not arrive at a settlement and reported that they could not agree. Most significantly, six teams made no report at all. Were they too ashamed to report their lack of progress?

When settlements were reached, the amounts ranged from $15,000 to a high of $95,000. The table below illustrates the results of this experiment.

Table 16.1
Results of Demand and Offer Study

Negotiating Team	Plaintiff's Opening Demands	Defendant's Opening Offer	Settlement Amount
1	$ 32,000	$ 10,000	$ 18,000
2	50,000	25,000	No Settlement
3	675,000	32,150	95,000
4	110,000	3,000	25,000
5	Not Reported	Not Reported	15,000
6	100,000	5,000	25,000
7	475,000	15,000	No Settlement
8	180,000	40,000	80,000
9	210,000	17,000	57,000
10	350,000	48,500	61,000
11	87,500	15,000	30,000
12	175,000	50,000	Narrowed to $137,000 - $ 77,000
13	97,000	10,000	57,000
14	100,000	Unknown	56,875

* Comments and table reprinted with permission of West Publishing Company from Legal Negotiation and Settlement by Gerald R. Williams.

As Professor Williams noted, "It is apparent that there were dramatic differences, not only in the perceptions these lawyers had about the value of the case, but in the persuasiveness or skill with which they pursued their objectives".

Professor Williams concluded, "The study raises questions about how well lawyers are able, under present methods, to serve their own clients and/or the public interest through negotiated settlements".

Why are negotiators, working from the same set of facts, often so far apart?

One reason may be the ritual of many lawyers and insurance representatives. For many, it is like the bargaining of a medieval bazaar: demand high, offer low; lower the demand a little, increase the offer a little; continue the bartering until the offer and demand meet. If they do not meet, the claim moves further into litigation and perhaps trial.

Even when the injured person's attorney knows what the case is worth, the thinking may be that to get a reasonable settlement, you have to ask for far more than you expect to get. This is consistent with the opening demands in Professor Williams' experiment.

Similar invalid "logic" may be guiding the insurance adjuster. There are insurance company personnel who take the position that it is a sign of weakness to approach the plaintiff's attorney about settling a case. They feel that they should not be approached, otherwise they will have to pay too much. The adjuster must deal with internal red tape. The adjuster's authority may be restricted by a supervisor, whose authority may be limited by the home office. As a result, such companies may make no effective effort to settle cases.

With neither side approaching the other with serious settlement proposals, nothing happens, except litigation.

Another reason negotiators may be so far apart is that they often rely on the litigation process to help them determine the value.

At a recent ABA meeting, a panel of judges and attorneys who specialize in personal injury litigation considered the question of runaway litigation. A number of judges pointed out that attorneys who knew very little about personal injury value were responsible for much of the tort litigation. Many of these attorneys eventually turned their cases over to personal injury specialists, but not until years had passed and they were facing the threat of the courtroom for trial.

Several of the judges noted that when the final trial date was set, many of the attorneys without trial experience and knowledge of cases panicked and advised their clients to settle for much less than the case was worth.

Even attorneys adept at handling personal injury claims may pursue litigation because they take the position that an insurance company will not pay the proper price without it. They have learned that all they have to do is enter suit and the offer goes up at every stage of the litigation process. Some hold out until the case is in trial. Some go a step further and figure the insurance company will come up with real money when a jury is staring them in the face. These attorneys make no sincere effort to settle until they enter the trial room, or empanel the jury. Talk of settlement by attorneys is really a charade. It is not meant to really settle a case, they are merely going through the motions until they enter the courtroom.

Letting the court procedure help resolve cases can take

years, and the results still may be quite different than if the case had been submitted to a jury.

Defense attorneys often do nothing to alleviate this problem. Unfortunately, the defense counsel who is being paid on an hourly basis doesn't really have any inducement to end profitable representation. While many defense attorneys do exert vigorous efforts to settle cases, the fact remains the same. Self-interest will often prevail. After all, the longer a case pend and the more court processes that are involved, the larger the defense attorney's fee.

Some defense attorneys now realize that this action is costly to their clients and can actually cause them to lose insurance clients.

The judiciary's leverage

While many attorneys and adjusters turn to the court system for assistance, a trial judge who presides over criminal trials, domestic relations and contract injunctions may not have much experience with personal injury jury trials. Hence, the judge's knowledge of value may differ little from that of the attorney who has never tried a case.

"Judges' direct experience of civil juries may be limited", Law Professor Marc Galanter observed in his 1990 paper, The Civil Jury as Regulator of the Litigation Process. "There are less than ten civil jury trials per judge annually in the federal system, and their features vary significantly to render elusive any useful generalizations".

Most judges sincerely want to help settle the cases assigned to them. This is particularly true since most jurisdictions now have individual dockets for which the judge is responsible. Unfortunately, most judges have little assistance. Even though the most important reason that cases enter and continue in litigation is because there is no agreement on what they are worth, few judges are provided with research information on value.

Although, court administrators also deplore the delay in the courts under their administration, few bother to tackle the problem at its cause.

Most state trial courts are under the jurisdiction of the state Supreme Court--usually the Chief Justice. They too issue reports deploring the long delay. However, aside from commending judges who efficiently handle their dockets and requesting that the legislature provide more judges, they also fail to address the central problem.

There are many knowledgeable judges who do an outstanding job of effecting equitable settlements. However, there are too few of them to effectively resolve every personal injury case on the docket.

Some judges may have an idea of the value, but may offer little or no assistance because of the political realities of elected judges. Attorneys are usually polled during election campaigns, and bar association endorsement depends on lawyer approval. As a result of these many factors, the court process often does little to help the unknowledgeable attorney settle his cases.

It is obvious that the so-called experience of most attorneys, insurance company adjusters and even claims supervisors with jury verdicts is limited. Their information is so limited, that their predictions can best be described as "the partially educated guess". This explains why personal injury valuations and predictions of jury verdicts differ so much from actual results, as is evident when their offers and demands are compared to verdict results.

The result of "the partially educated guess"

The partially educated guess obviously leads to large gaps between what the attorneys for the plaintiff and the attorneys defense think the case is worth. It also leads to large gaps in what they think the jury think the case is worth.

This is clearly illustrated by a recent study of personal injury verdicts by Jury Verdict Research in which liability was not an issue and the final demand and/or final offer was reported.

The final demands in 37 percent of the cases were less than the juries awarded. Many were only a fraction of the ultimate verdicts in the cases. The following were the first six cases listed in the research report:

Demand	Verdict
$100,000	$4,947,860
33,000	900,000
5,000	100,000
100,000	1,650,000
250,000	4,100,000

These were not the only cases in which demands missed the verdicts by sizable amounts, there were many more.

Of the cases in which lower demands were rejected by the insurer, 21 percent were no more than three-quarters of the size of the ultimate verdicts.

This may be the tip of the iceberg. Many cases settle in the courtroom and lawyer's office. This raises an important question. In how many settlements does the insurance company pass up modest demands? There is plenty of evidence that carriers spurn reasonable demands and enter into needless litigation too often, only to be greeted by verdicts many times larger than the demand. This can affect the insurance premiums that everyone pays.

Of the final offers in the study, 28 percent were larger than the verdicts, and 11 percent of these were two to six times greater! Again, this is the tip of the iceberg of offers much larger than corresponding verdicts. In these cases, the plaintiff attorneys turned down offers and pursued costly litigation only to earn less money for themselves and their clients.

While one cannot expect all final demands or offers to be the same size as the verdicts. To be considered sound they should fall within the statistical probability range. This is a range 25 percent higher and 25 percent lower than the actual verdict. For example, the probability range for a $100,000 verdict is $75,000 (25 percent below) to $125,000 (25 percent above).

This study revealed that only 18 percent of the final demands and 17 percent of the offers were within the appropriate probability range. Only two percent of the demands and two percent of the offers were equal to the verdicts. This is a sad finding, especially since lawyers and insurance companies generally make their best predictions when facing the finality of a jury decision.

The study of final demands and offers did not include the 37 percent of verdicts which are delivered for the defense, only those cases where the juries awarded money. It must not be overlooked that in 37 to 40 percent of all cases, the juries find for the defendants and the injured plaintiffs get nothing.

However, the chance of the injured person losing the case varies dramatically depending on the specific situation. For example, plaintiffs lose 70 percent of the automobile cases in which they were pulling out of a driveway. In products liability cases involving buses, plaintiffs lose 80 percent of the cases that juries decide. On the other hand, in rear-end collision cases, defense verdicts account for only 27 percent of the verdicts.

Under comparative negligence laws, in addition to deciding the value of the injury, the jury decides how much each party was at fault. Was the defendant careless (negligent), and if so, to what extent did it cause the plaintiff's injuries? Did the injured person contribute to his/her own injuries, and if so, to what extent? Applying the laws of such states, which are somewhat complicated and vary from state to state, judges found another ten percent of the injured were not entitled to any compensation.

Determining who will win is as important as predicting verdict size. Since defendants win so many cases, it is important that attorneys and insurance personnel accurately predict whether the jury will find in favor of the plaintiff.

Studies show that in most of the defense verdict cases, offers had been made, and they were often sizable.

In a case that involved a young boy in a bicycle accident, the defense offered $750,000 for the boy's brain damage and paraplegia, but the jury awarded nothing because it found the boy contributorily negligent.

This clearly indicates that the trial lawyer representing the injured, based on past "experience," wrongly predicted a victory, and that the victory would bring more than the final offer. Yet, the jury awarded nothing. Obviously, the lawyer representing an injured person who relies solely on past "experience" can be very costly to clients. However, for over 30 years recovery probability tables have been available to guide the attorneys and insurance carriers.

Conclusion

Every insurance executive, risk manager and attorney representing either the injured or defendant knows that our personal injury compensation system is a jury system. Yet, surprisingly few attorneys and insurance carriers bother to supplement their own limited experience with information about what juries do in different liability and injury situations, in spite of the fact that injury verdict probabilities with the same validity as life expectancy probabilities have been available for over 30 years.

Lawyers are advocates and there is nothing wrong with getting their clients as large a settlement as possible or with the insurance company saving as much as possible while still being fair. Both are professionals looking out for the best interests of their clients. However, when negotiating conduct prevents a reasonable, prompt settlement, neither is serving the true needs of their clients.

#15

Public Officials Who Promise You Lower Insurance Costs By Setting Rates Are A Major Cause Of The Game

Candidates for public offices, insurance commissioners, and self-appointed citizens promise to save you money by regulating automobile insurance rates. They promise to roll back insurance premiums. Since most voters own an automobile and want lower premiums, the candidates with such promises often get elected.

Unfortunately, insurance rate regulation promises work as well as the promises of communism. Communism promised that by regulating the economies they would deliver more goods to the people. It is now clear by destroying their market economies and competition, they delivered much less.

The countries that provided "market economies" and thus competition have done far better for their citizens.

The policyholders in states that do not set insurance rates have the lowest cost insurance and a greater choice of coverage. In the states that set rates, insurance costs their policyholders more and their choices are limited. Even careful drivers find themselves in assigned risk pools. "The most blatant examples of misguided regulatory involvement in automobile insurance prices occurred in Massachusetts and New Jersey". Jean C. Hiestand, the V.P. General Counsel of State Farm Insurance Company, in Competition And The Rating Laws: Do They Make A Difference? "They not only pay the highest rates but a large percentage are in involuntary markets".

Hiestand continues, "If such regulatory interference persists over time, the market can be changed drastically for the worse, perhaps permanently. The demise of the New Jersey and Massachusetts auto insurance markets provides a dramatic warning of this danger. The studies demonstrate clearly that open competition yields lower costs, fair prices for the consumer and greater availability of the product to the consumer".

"Over the years, in states where the forces of competition have been allowed to operate, they have fulfilled the basic promises of the competitive model, cost based prices fairly reflecting changes in supply and demand, new product innovation, and the rewards of increased market share to efficient, high quality competitors who offer attractive products at fair prices".

A 1977 Department of Justice study noted that rate regulation results in "aggravation of the availability problem, particularly for marginal or high insurance risks; financial instability in some insurance company operations; cross-subsidization between low and high insurance risks, and unwarranted restrictions on collective merchandising and direct writing of insurance. Sadly, the experience of auto insurers demonstrates there are very few states in which competition is permitted to govern rates fully".

Cross subsidization between low and high insurance risks means that the careful drivers pay higher rates so the careless drivers pay less.

Insurance rate regulation has created a "cost plus operation". For this reason there is little incentive for the insurance companies to control costs.

This "cost plus" operation, unfortunately, spills over to

the handling of claims and costs. The result: some insurance companies will pay more than they should, in settling their claims. Insurance companies spread their losses as much as possible. Hence, drivers in non-regulated states may be covering the losses in regulated states. (One state recently passed a law forbidding this practice.)

When insurance companies lost money in only a few states because of rate setting, this could be done. As more states regulate rates, and insurance companies have fewer profitable states, these losses could no longer be spread to the drivers of other states. The only choice was to stop writing automobile insurance in the unprofitable states.

If we got rid of state regulation of insurance rates and allowed competition to flower, the market would drive down insurance costs; an important factor in ending the 96 billion dollar game.

Even in states where automobile premiums are highly regulated, an important class of casualty insurance it is difficult to set rates. This is insurance covering businesses of different sizes, products and services, operating in many states and foreign countries. These defy even the most ardent regulators. So, in most states, business casualty insurance rates are not effectively regulated. Rate competition for such insurance in these states is intense.

Risk managers who shop around find they can save thousands and even millions of dollars. The problem created is that to book such businesses, insurers often set the premiums too low. This may affect the company's profitability, and perhaps even its solvency. State insurance commissioners watch for this. This is an important part of their job. Careful risk managers in selecting insurers, check on their financial stability. After all, the purpose of competition is to make insurers as efficient as possible, not to guarantee the profitability of business insurers. If some fail the test, so be it. If a failed insurer also insures automobile owners, every state has a guarantee fund to take care of them.

#16

Betting The Odds: Jury Information Leads To Fair Settlement

A poker player who bets the odds wins in the long run. An opponent's occasional lucky draw may dampen a winning streak, but going with the odds will cut loses and produce winners more consistently than luck or flying by the seat of your pants.

The same is true in the personal injury game. When players rely on luck and the partially educated guess, they and everyone around them pay. This is evident by the overall high cost of litigating claims, the non-productive nature of most litigation and the individual cost to everyone involved.

The key to avoiding this entire scenario is for attorneys and insurance companies to arrive at settlement values that are based on fact, are valid and acceptable to all parties. Injured victims with legitimate negligence claims should receive equitable compensation without the cost and delay of litigation. Insurance carriers should be able to save money by being cooperative and promptly compensating deserving claimants. Attorneys who represent claimants should receive reasonable compensation for their services. Defense attorneys should be able to market their litigation expertise for cases that warrant expertise. Policyholders who support the system should have market leverage for assuring its efficiency based upon open competition. Politicians and commissioners who legislate the system should support our market economy by allowing competition to set the price for service and coverage. This may sound impossible, but quite frankly the process for achieving all of these goals is logical, practical and attainable if a few basic guidelines are followed.

The first is to respect the role of juries in setting the market price of cases for personal injury negotiation and resolution. That information can be integrated into the personal injury system voluntarily by attorneys and insurance carriers and through social and economic leverage by the public.

Juries set the market

Everyone involved in personal injury, from the insurance company to the injured person, talk in terms of what a jury would do if it heard the case. It's not only the gossip at the local diner, it is the discussion at the law firm conference room and negotiations on the courthouse steps.

In Settled Out of Court: The Social Process of Insurance Claims Adjustment, H. Lawrence Ross discovered that, "the basis of settlement in serious cases, seems on both sides to be an estimate of the likely recovery of the claimant before a jury. Both sides came to this estimate by comparing a given case in its many dimensions against similar cases that have gone to trial".

Marc Galanter, professor of law and director of the Disputes Processing Research Program at the University of Wisconsin, is widely recognized as a leading authority on juries and the American System of Civil Litigation. In his 1990 paper "The Civil Jury As Regulator Of The Litigation Process", Professor Galanter noted that: "The relative importance of juries as transmitters of signals rather than deciders of cases seems to have increased in recent years".

Since juries make the final decisions and their actions clearly drive the negotiating process, knowing how juries react to different issues is crucial in the efficient resolution of claims.

Juries follow patterns in their awards for similar injuries with similar economic loss

Since everyone talks in terms of what a jury would do with a case, they essentially set a value for personal injury claims. To determine the value of a case, it is crucial to be able to predict with a reasonable probability a jury's decision.

To see if verdicts were actually predictable, researchers at Jury Verdict Research analyzed cases involving cervical strain popularly referred to as "whiplash" in 1961. Several hundred verdicts in cases which the injured people had similar medical expenses and lost wages were gathered.

First, verdicts in cases with medical expense and lost wages ranging from $24 to $199 were surveyed. The study showed that one-third of the verdicts in these cases were within a $500 range. With this positive indication, additional verdicts were collected from rural and metropolitan areas throughout the United States. More than 10,000 verdicts were collected. This represented almost one-third of the personal injury verdicts which were rendered in the U.S. in a year, so it was clearly a sufficient sampling. In the expanded study, half of the verdicts were within $500 of each other, indicating that most of the verdicts were clustering within a range.

The following charts illustrate the results of these two studies.

Table 12.1
Cervical Strain Verdicts
$24 to $199 Expense Classifications

Preliminary Study | **Expanded Study**

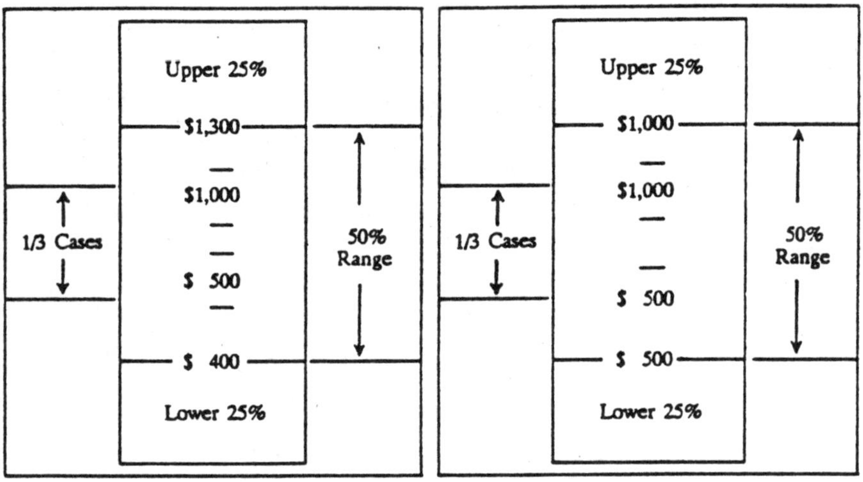

The same process was applied to slightly more serious cases. Those with medical expense and wage loss ranging from $200 to $499, again, the study showed that one-third of the verdicts were within a $500 range of one another. When the number of verdicts were expanded, one-half of the verdicts were within $500 of each other.

The following charts illustrate the results of cases with medical expense and wage loss between $200 and $499.

Table 12.2
Cervical Strain Verdicts
$200 to $499 Expense Classifications

Preliminary study | **Expanded study**

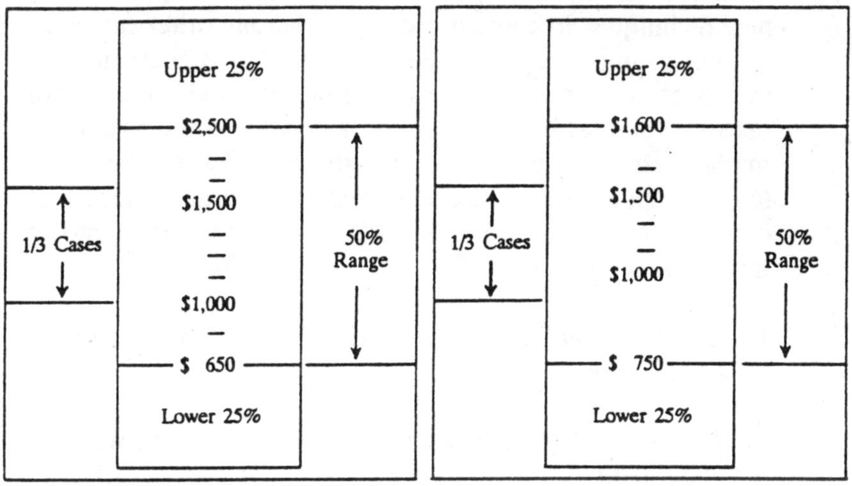

These studies confirmed that verdicts for similar injuries with similar economic loss follow patterns, tending to cluster within a range. Since they cluster around the middle or midpoint verdict, that cluster can be predicted.

With this confirmation, injury value tables were prepared for all injuries. The tables were tested by comparing them to jury trial results in similar cases. The tests showed that the tables were valid and could be used to determine the probable verdict size for any injury. These tables have also been used successfully for over 30 years by many attorneys and insurance companies further proving their validity

The value of any given injury can change over time and some injuries may be affected more than others. Changes are most likely influenced by inflation, medical developments and new techniques in court presentation among other factors.

For example, as medical treatment of particular injuries improves, jury awards for such injuries tend to diminish because the cost of treatment goes down and the long term medical effect is diminished. On the other hand, as more is learned about the nature and true long term disability of certain other injuries, jury awards for these injuries tend to increase accordingly.

Juries follow predictable patterns in deciding fault or liability in similar types of cases

Jurors are also consistent when they are deciding whether the defendant is guilty of negligence. Of all the personal injury verdicts rendered throughout the country in 1959, jurors found for the plaintiffs 60 percent of the time. This rate has varied only slightly in 30 years and today it is 63 percent.

For many kinds of accidents there has been little or no change. For example, 30 years ago jurors found for defendants 23 percent of the time when hearing rear-end collision cases. Today defendants win 27 percent of the time.

In 1960, premises liability cases like falls in grocery stores, jurors found for the injured parties 50 percent of the time. Ten years ago the injured person received an award in 52 percent of all premises liability cases. Today, injured people still win 52 percent of these cases.

In 1978, students injured in playground accidents received an award in 55 percent of the cases. Today, they win 58 percent of the verdicts.

Actuarial figures can be adjusted for the specifics of any personal injury case

Probability tables are very similar to the life expectancy tables used by insurance companies to set the price of life insurance. When you purchase a life insurance policy, the insurance company knows how long a person with your characteristics can be expected to live. While some policyholders may be hit by a car the next day, others may live many years longer than expected. However, these are the exceptions.

Over the years, life expectancy tables have proven to be a very reliable way of helping to set life insurance policy rates. Life insurance companies have learned how to refine their methods to consider someone's individual health. Life insurance companies often require physical examinations. If the applicant has heart problems or high blood pressure, the company will take that into consideration when setting the premium. Often the size of the premium will be increased according to the mathematical risk involved with the person's health. On the other hand, certain insurance companies recognize that non-smokers live longer and will charge them a lower rate.

Likewise, verdict figures can be adjusted to take into account the specific facts of a case. Where the trial would be held will affect the value because awards are higher in some states than in others. If the facts are being disputed, the award is often lower. Even the age and sex of the plaintiff or defendant can affect the jury's decision.

Predicting jury verdicts

This research proved that juries are predictable and that information could be used to predict the probable outcome for individual cases. Negotiators can look at not only the amount that a jury would probably award the injured, but also at their chance of receiving a favorable verdict. In rear-end collision cases, if the probable verdict size is $10,000 and the chance of losing is 27 percent, the actuarial value is $7,300. This is the value at the point of but just before a jury's verdict because of the factors and the risk involved.

Jury Verdict Research, Inc. (JVR), an impartial and internationally recognized research company has been collecting and verifying reports of personal injury verdicts throughout the United States for over 30 years. The verdicts are analyzed by researchers and statisticians who compute tables of injury values. Verdict expectancy tables show the verdict value of injury claims. Recovery probability tables show the odds of a jury finding for the injured plaintiff.

The point of demonstrating the predictability of verdicts is to illustrate a workable method of settling personal injury cases. Rather than relying on luck and the partially educated guess, attorneys and insurance companies can use research tables as a valid means of predicting the verdict size and outcome. It is just like betting the odds. Reiterating the role of the jury, Professor Galanter of the University of Wisconsin Law School stated:

> "Most cases will continue to be resolved in the jury's shadow rather than by the jury itself. But some shadows are more distinct, readable and current than others. Just as the decisions of professionals may be degraded, so may the currency of jury decisions be debased. In considering the future of the jury, we must think of it not only as a decider of disputes, but as a producer of signals for the operation of the system of settlements".

But knowing the jury's verdict is the first step in the settlement process.

Litigation costs affect the settlement value

Verdict research helps decipher the jury signals that Professor Galanter talks about, but there are two additional elements involved in determining the value of a case when talking in terms of settlement. These are litigation costs and the effect of litigation delay. Getting to the point of a verdict requires many years, many hours of attorney time and often substantial litigation expenses. These all affect the bottom-line of a verdict.

The costs of litigating a case can dramatically cut the net recovery of both the injured party and the attorney. And since these expenses are avoided with an early settlement, essentially they do not need to be recovered when the case is settled early.

Until recently, no one knew exactly how much it would cost to litigate an individual case or what economic effect the years spent in litigation would have on the parties. As a result, one could only guess at the value of a claim before a lawsuit was filed.

A formula to help determine early settlement value was obviously needed and under my direction, Jury Verdict Research, Inc. undertook research to develop such a formula.

The first step was the cost accounting of a variety of personal injury cases. For each case, the lawyer's expenses were obtained and analyzed, including out-of-pocket expenses filing fees, expert witness fees, travel costs, exhibits, etc., law firm overhead for the case and the salaries of secretaries, paralegals and associate lawyers. The hourly fee of the law firm partner or sole proprietor was not included, however, the overhead costs required for them to work were included. The partner and the sole proprietor are not paid an hourly rate so their costs were not included. They earn what is left after all other expenses are paid.

When these cases and costs were analyzed, statisticians found a relationship ratio between the litigation costs and probable verdict size. This was used as a basis for determining litigation costs for similar cases. The formula was repeatedly tested and proven to be valid.

Researchers then discovered that by subtracting these litigation costs from the probable verdict amount and adjusting for the chance of losing the case, they arrived at a fair settlement value. The basic settlement value was fair because it was approximately the same amount that plaintiff and representing counsel would have received after expenses if the case had been submitted to a jury within one year of filing a lawsuit. This comparison takes into account economic factors like inflation and the ability to earn interest.

Since an injured person deserves to have an efficient attorney, the most efficient use of an attorney's time was used as the basis for arriving at a uniform Basic Settlement Value. This is particularly important since the formula for settlement value deducts litigation costs from the verdict. The more efficient the attorney, the smaller the deduction and the larger the settlement value. This clearly benefits the injured person.

From a practical standpoint, the limits of the defendant's insurance policy may affect the ability to collect a settlement therefore, affecting the settlement amount. If more than one person is injured by the same driver, the total value of the cases may exceed the available policy limit. Accordingly, the Basic Settlement Value would have to be reduced to fit within the available insurance coverage.

Time lapse affects settlement value

Since it takes years to litigate to a verdict, the effect of that time must be considered when comparing settlement results with possible verdict results. Time affects both the cost of litigating and the value of recovery. The specific economic factors, the decrease in purchasing power due to inflation, the interest potential lost due to a delay in receiving compensation, the increase in the time required to handle litigation, the increase in litigation costs, the interest potential lost on expense outlays and the annual increase in verdict value were outlined in Chapter 11 when we talked about the delay in the court system and its effect on cases.

These economic influences are important because they increase the long term value of a settlement received today. At the same time, they decrease the value of money received in the future.

In a jurisdiction where it takes six months after filing a lawsuit to reach trial, the effect of interest and inflation is very different from a jurisdiction in which it takes five years.

In six months, the injured person loses six months of interest, incurs six months of lost purchasing power due to inflation and a possible increase in litigation costs. Consequently, the injured person's attorney and insurance carrier will have increases in litigation costs.

However, where the case will take five years, the difference is going to be very large due to the loss of interest, loss of purchasing power, and increased cost of litigation.

The result is that the value of two injury cases with the same liability situation will be vastly different. These are illustrated more specifically in Chapters 17 and 18 where a sample case is presented.

Affecting change in the system

Knowing that the settlement value of a claim can be determined, based on the odds, is the first step in converting the system from an inefficient system to a cost effective one. Armed with this knowledge, progressive attorneys and insurance companies can immediately begin to improve their own performance. Both policyholders and injured clients will benefit.

Armed with this information, policyholders and clients can

take steps to make sure they are part of the group benefiting from the effective use of this information.

The use of verdict and economic information in the negotiation of individual cases is presented in Chapters 17 and 18 followed by its importance in the selection of insurance companies and attorneys.

#17

The Ace In The Hole: Information

Information is abundant in today's high-tech society. Instant satellite communications and computers that can store and process billions of pieces of information have put the world at our fingertips.

Personal injury litigation is no exception. The general consumer is bombarded with media coverage of verdicts, insurance policyholder revolts, product liability crises and medical malpractice epidemics.

The players in the system are exposed to at least a half dozen national trade publications that analyze every angle of tort law and insurance coverage. Just about every state has local publications that report verdicts. Also, an ever growing number of consultants, economists, research companies and experts who sell their ability to analyze individual cases. Attorneys and insurance adjusters are swimming in a sea of information.

This information is enhanced by the growing use of computer technology in insurance companies and law firms. Price Waterhouse recently surveyed law firms and found that two-thirds of the firms said they would increase per lawyer spending on technology in 1991.

The new challenge is to effectively integrate this influx of information and technology into the negotiating system. As Professor Galanter pointed out in his report:

> "As the structures of professional life are

> altered, the sources of information about juries are changing. With fewer jury trials relative to the number of cases and to the number of lawyers, lawyers have less direct personal experience with juries. New channels of information proliferate, making available a flow of information that is both richer and harder to interpret. Improved education, greater specialization, the nationalization of law practice, the upgrading of the plaintiffs' bar all change the ways in which this information is processed. The arrival of voluminous and detailed systematic research on juries means there is both more "good" and "bad" jury information around. Lawyers now must add skill in doping out research to skill in doping out juries".

By entering the information age, negotiators can significantly improve the negligence system by avoiding unnecessary, non-productive litigation and settling their cases more effectively.

Knowing how this can be done, policyholders, consumers and injured victims have the first weapon in their arsenal. They have the information needed to assure that their money is being spent wisely, their rights are being protected and their system of justice is being respected.

Like the poker player who has an ace in the hole, the negotiator with the right information in hand is prepared to win in negotiations and serve the best interests of their clients, whether they are defendants, insurance policyholders or injured litigants.

The key verdict values of any case should be determined

Knowing that past jury decisions are predictors of future jury decisions, the first step in integrating information into the negotiation process is to predict what a jury would likely do with each individual case.

Many insurance companies, attorneys representing the injured, defense attorneys and self-insured companies have been relying on verdict information to price personal injury cases.

Those who have not are relying on "the partially educated guess". Men and women like yourself who pay the premiums that support this system, can expect that their own insurance companies will minimize the cost of insurance by using such information in the pricing of personal injury cases.

The first step in assuring prompt, fair settlement is for each negotiator to determine what would probably happen if the case were tried to a verdict. The probable verdict amount and the probability of a plaintiff verdict are the two key values. Since many settlements take place in the courtroom before a verdict is delivered, it is important to know the value of the case at that point. This is based upon the probable verdict amount factored by the chance of winning.

The following example illustrates the type of information available for individual cases. As you can see, the value of the injury, the plaintiff's chance of recovery and the effect of specific case facts are predicted. These values are a result of the analytical process outlined in the previous chapter.

This is an automobile case involving an intersection

collision at a four way stop. The plaintiff, a 41 year old woman broke her wrist and nose in the accident.

DETERMINING VERDICT VALUE

Item	Recovery Rate	Injury Value
LIABILITY		
Intersection, 4-way stop	68%	
INJURY		
Wrist fracture and nose fracture		$42,271
Medical expense: $4,000		
Lost Wages: $800		
CASE SPECIFIC ADJUSTMENT		
Permanent pain and weakness	0%	3%
Female plaintiff age 40-49	-5%	7%
Cuyahoga County, Ohio	0%	4%
Total adjustments to injury value		14%
Total injury value		$48,189
Total adjustments to recovery rate	-5%	
PROBABLE VERDICT AMOUNT		**$50,000**
PROBABILITY OF PLAINTIFF VERDICT	**64%**	
ACTUAL VERDICT VALUE		$32,000
Actual verdict range		
Low		$24,000
Midpoint		$32,000
High		$48,000

This example takes the facts of the case and reports how a jury is likely to react to each fact. Based only on the type of accident, an intersection collision at a four-way stop, the chance of winning is 68 percent. Based only on the type of injury and severity, the injury value is $42,271. However, there are several other factors that will affect the jury's decision, including the plaintiff's claim that she is permanently impaired by the injury, the age and sex of the plaintiff and the location of the trial. These case facts adjust the value of the plaintiff's injury to $48,189 and her likelihood of winning to 64 percent. Since juries tend to round off awards, the probable verdict is $50,000.

The bottom-line of each party should be determined

The goal is to arrive at a fair settlement of each case early in the process saving policyholders, taxpayers and consumers billions of dollars in litigation costs. With this in mind, these verdict values become a first step in the settlement process. It costs the plaintiff and the attorney thousands of dollars to litigate to a verdict. Since those expenses would be avoided with an early settlement, they can feasibly recover that much less and still reach the same bottom-line without the risk of losing.

Knowing litigation costs, negotiators can determine the **Settlement Value** based on facts, the verdict value, the cost to litigate to the courtroom and the chance of winning not the partially educated guess.

In this same intersection collision, the following shows how the settlement value can be computed, using the analysis outlined in Chapter 16.

DETERMINING SETTLEMENT VALUE

Probable verdict amount	$50,000
Total litigation costs	- 7,934
Net value (at plaintiff verdict)	$42,066
Probability (of plaintiff verdict)	x 64%
BASIC SETTLEMENT VALUE	**$26,922**

Once the verdict value and settlement value has been determined, the plaintiff's share, plaintiff attorney's fee and insurance carrier's cost need to be determined. This requires some basic cost accounting. By doing this for each possible outcome, each player can see how they would fair with an early settlement, a settlement in the courtroom, a plaintiff verdict and a defense verdict.

To provide a true picture, this accounting must take into account all of the costs and how they affect each party's bottom-line. With this information, each party can compare different scenarios and know the best route for the claim.

The following chart shows the bottom-line for the plaintiff.

PLAINTIFF'S SHARE

EARLY SETTLEMENT	
Basic settlement value	$26,922
Out-of-pocket costs prior to suit	- 637
Net settlement amount	26,285
Attorney fees, 33 percent	- 8,673
Plaintiff Share	17,612
Personal Cost	- 100
Net Share	**17,512**
SETTLEMENT AT THE POINT OF A VERDICT	
Probable verdict amount	$50,000
Out-of-pocket costs	- 4,686
Value at plaintiff verdict	45,314
Probability of defense verdict, 36%	16,313
Value at point of verdict	29,001
Attorney Fees	- 9,570
Plaintiff share	19,431
Personal cost	- 526
Net share	18,905
PLAINTIFF VERDICT	
Probable verdict amount	$50,000
Out-of-pocket costs	- 4,686
Net verdict	45,314
Attorney fees	-14,954
Plaintiff share	30,360
Personal cost	- 526
Net share	**29,834**
DEFENSE VERDICT	
Personal costs	- 526

With a prompt settlement, the injured will get $17,512 after paying out-of-pocket costs, attorney's fee and personal expenses. If settled at the point of verdict, the injured person's share would be $18,905 after paying all expenses and factoring in the chance of losing. If the injured wins a plaintiff verdict, reimburses out-of-pocket costs, pays attorney fees and personal costs, a net share of $29,834 would be realized. To lose would cost him $526.

The effect of time should be calculated

At this point, these numbers show that an early settlement may not be the best result for the plaintiff. One very important fact is missing and that is how long it will take to actually receive the money and how it will affect his bottom-line. This is important because of the long delay to trial in many jurisdictions.

Local lawyers who are active in court can estimate when a case may go to trial. Unfortunately, in most jurisdictions the time to trial may vary from months to years for the individual case. Some lawyers attract or try so many cases that it may take years because of their backlog before your case reach a trial room. Other lawyers procrastinate and are never ready unless prodded by a strong judge. Parties, witnesses, lawyers, and judges may become ill, causing further delays. Criminal cases have priority and an overworked judge may have to postpone his personal injury cases for months. So it is important to compare the value of money received anywhere from one to nine years down the road. If there is credible evidence of the average length of time it takes for a case to reach trial in any one jurisdiction, that figure should be given the utmost consideration, but it cannot be relied upon.

The plaintiff and his attorney need to know how time will affect their recovery. The future value of settlement shows how much they can earn if they accept an early settlement and invest it. On the other hand, present value takes into account that a settlement or verdict in the trial court may be after many years of litigation. During that time, the value of the injury will go up, but this increase is more than offset by growing litigation costs, the lost purchasing power of the dollar and lost investment earnings. All of these are taken into consideration in calculating present value of a verdict or settlement to the plaintiff or the plaintiff's attorney. If a defense verdict is delivered, the plaintiff team's expenses will have increased annually over time with no recovery to offset them.

The following chart shows the time spent in litigation and how it affects the plaintiff's money.

THE EFFECT OF LITIGATION DELAY
ON THE PLAINTIFF'S SHARE

Year	Early Settlement Future Value 8.375%	Point Of Verdict Present Value -6.360%	Plaintiff Verdict Present Value -6.360%	Defense Verdict Annual Increase 11.153%
1	$17,511	$18,905	$29,834	$-526
2	20,567	16,576	26,160	-650
3	22,290	15,522	24,496	-722
4	24,156	14,535	22,938	-803
5	26,179	13,611	21,479	-892
6	28,372	12,745	20,113	-992
7	30,748	11,934	18,834	-1,103
8	33,323	11,175	17,636	-1,226
9	36,114	10,465	16,515	-1,362

In three years, the net share from an early settlement has grown to $22,290 and the value of the plaintiff's share from a settlement at the point of a verdict has decreased to $15,522. Note that a plaintiff verdict has decreased in value to $24,496.

At the end of four years, which is not an uncommon wait for trial, the settlement would be worth more than a plaintiff verdict of $24,156 versus $22,938.

This final step clearly shows the advantage of an early settlement for the injured litigant. It gives negotiators the fact-based information they need to reach prompt settlements that are fair to all of the parties.

This analysis can be performed for each party to the claim. To clean up litigation, this information needs to be used effectively in negotiations, which is the subject of the next chapter.

#18

The Wild Card: Marketing

Winning! That's the goal in poker and in negotiations. Just as the wild card gives a poker player an advantage, marketing gives a negotiator an advantage. Because we live in a bottom-line society, everyone wants to know the bottom line: "What's in it for me?" or "What do I stand to lose?" This is the driving force behind the sale of any product, service or idea.

In personal injury negotiations, the product is settlement. Players have to sell settlement to the opposing side. As with any sale, the emphasis must be a benefit to the buyer. Being able to show the opposing party or litigant the advantage of an early settlement is selling him the benefit.

Attorneys and insurance companies who use information to prove the validity of their settlement offers or demands and illustrate the costly effect of litigation on the opposing party's bottom-line can expect to get prompt and fair settlements.

The cost accounting outline in the previous chapter can be done for each party to a claim. As with the injured person, analysis repeatedly shows the benefit of settling claims early. The plaintiff attorney makes more money and the insurance company saves a substantial amount of money in both litigation costs and claim costs when reasonable settlements are reached early in the negotiating game.

Marketing will assist to bring settlement information to the attention of negotiators.

Marketing to the injured party

The printout in the previous chapter is perfect for the insurance adjuster or the plaintiff attorney to show the injured person the benefit of early settlement, taking into account the length of time they will have to wait to recover from litigation.

However, the long term outlook may not be the only thing that motivates the injured person. The claimant may need money immediately and not want to wait out litigation even if there is a one in a million or a 50 percent chance for the big verdict. Many people simply want to be done with the unpleasant experience of being injured and having to wade through the insurance quagmire.

People are often nervous about uncertainty or the unknown and are willing to take a sure thing now as opposed to a settlement in the future. Since nearly 40 percent of the people who gamble on a jury trial lose and get nothing, this is also an important fact that can be used to bring home the value of settling. Actual examples of cases similar to the plaintiff's can also be effective for illustrating the possible negative result of trial, thereby improving the positive perception of early settlement.

Many injured people will be satisfied with the piece of mind they receive from reimbursement of medical expenses, lost income and sensible compensation for their pain and suffering.

In any case, the insurance adjuster must be careful not to take advantage of the injured person by making a less than fair settlement. It can come back to haunt the company if a plaintiff attorney is made aware of the case and brings bad faith charges against the company. Most insurance claim executives insist that their claim adjusters be fair with the injured claimant.

Marketing to the plaintiff attorney

Obviously, lawyers are concerned with the welfare of their clients, but let us be realistic. They have to maintain their firm, their own standard of living and they are also concerned with their own bottom-line. In the same sample case presented in the previous chapter, the plaintiff attorney nets more income with a settlement before a suit is filed than with a plaintiff verdict. Because of the attorney's office overhead and salaries, litigation is often a losing proposition.

The following chart picks up the same case outlined in Chapter 17, except it shows the costs for the injured's attorney.

PLAINTIFF COUNSEL'S FEE

EARLY SETTLEMENT	
Basic settlement value	$26,922
Out-of-pocket costs prior to suit	- 637
Net settlement amount	$26,285
Plaintiff share, 67%	-17,611
Attorney's fee 33%	8,674
Expenses	- 1,160
Net fee	7,514
SETTLEMENT AT THE POINT OF A VERDICT	
Probable verdict amount	$50,000
Out-of-pocket costs	- 4,686
Value at plaintiff verdict	45,314
Probability of def. verdict 36%	-16,313
Value at point of verdict	29,001
Plaintiff share	-19,431
Attorney's fee	9,570
Expense	- 7,926
Net fee	1,644
PLAINTIFF VERDICT	
Probable verdict amount	$50,000
Out-of-pocket costs	- 4,686
Net verdict	45,314
Plaintiff share	-30,360
Attorney's fee	14,954
Expenses	- 7,926
Net fee	**7,028**
DEFENSE VERDICT	
Expenses	- 7,926

Clearly, this information is something the insurance carrier can use to sell settlement to the plaintiff attorney. With an early settlement, the attorney makes $500 more than if a plaintiff verdict is won **and there is no risk.** By taking the risk and losing, the $7,926 spent on office overhead, staff salaries and out-of-pocket costs is lost. The plaintiff attorney may not be aware of how much it will cost to litigate the case and how dramatically the costs will affect that all important bottom-line. Between this information and the information itemizing the injured person's share, the defense attorney or the adjuster can sell settlement.

If this information doesn't do the trick, the insurance carrier can show the attorney how the years spent in litigation will further dissipate any fees awarded.

THE EFFECT OF LITIGATION DELAY ON THE PLAINTIFF ATTORNEY'S FEE

Year Increase	Early Settlement Future Value 8.375%	Point Of Verdict Present Value -9.253%	Plaintiff Verdict Present Value -9.253%	Defense Verdict Annual Increase 14.179%
	$7,514	$ 1,644	$ 7,028	$-7,926
1	8,143	1,492	6,377	-9,066
2	8,825	1,345	5,787	-10,369
3	9,565	1,229	5,252	-11,860
4	10,366	1,115	4,766	-13,566
5	11,234	1,012	4,325	-15,516
6	12,175	918	3,925	-17,747
7	13,194	833	3,562	-20,299
8	14,299	756	3,232	-23,218
9	15,497	686	2,933	-26,556

If the attorney reaches an early settlement and invests it for three years, that money will nearly double than what an award from a plaintiff verdict would be worth after three years of litigation. Even more disturbing, during the same three years, inflation will have kicked the potential loss from a defense verdict to $11,860.

Marketing to the insurance company or self-insurer

Paying an attorney to defend a claim can double an insurer's cost. This fact alone may compel the bill paying insurer, whether it is a traditional insurance company or a corporation that is insuring itself to look more seriously at a settlement demand. The insurer has very little to look forward to in litigation, either a defense verdict or one much lower than the final demand. While there is always a chance of a defense verdict, it is only a 37 to 40 percent chance overall. Meanwhile, the insurer's expenses continue to mount and the value of the claim continues to climb.

Cost accounting of the same case illustrates just how much the insurer risks in litigation. This table picks up after the calculation of the $26,922 settlement value.

DEFENSE COSTS

Early Settlement	
Net Cost at Settlement	$26,922
Settlement at the Point of a Verdict	
Probable Verdict Amount	$50,000
Expenses	+14,742
Cost at Plaintiff Verdict	64,742
Probable of Plaintiff Verdict	x 64%
Net Cost	41,435
Plaintiff Verdict	
Probable Verdict Amount	$50,000
Expenses	+14,742
Net Cost	64,742
Defense	$14,742

A plaintiff verdict will cost the insurer over double what the early settlement would cost. There is always the risk that the jury will award more than the norm. Yes, the insurer can appeal that outcome, but at what cost? Just look at the long term effect of litigation for the cost of one claim without an appeal.

THE EFFECT OF LITIGATION DELAY ON DEFENSE COSTS

Year	Early Settlement	Point of Verdict Annual Increase 11.720%	Plaintiff Verdict Annual Increase 11.720%	Defense Verdict Annual Increase 9.360%
	$26,922	$41,435	$64,742	$14,742
1		46,291	72,330	16,122
2		51,716	80,807	17,631
3		57,788	90,277	19,281
4		64,549	100,858	21,086
5		72,114	112,678	23,059
6		80,566	125,884	25,218
7		90,008	140,638	27,578
8		100,557	157,121	30,160
9		112,343	175,535	32,982

Looking at the long term effect of litigation, even a defense verdict is not that appealing. After only a few years in litigation, "winning" a defense verdict will cost nearly $20,000. Even though the insurer is required to put aside the value of the claim in a reserve, the interest earned is not enough to offset these inflationary increases.

The compounding effect and costs if the case is settled in court or the plaintiff wins, is a very scary prospect for the insurer. Each year the resolution is delayed, the insurer can expect to spend another $5,000 to $10,000.

Marketing through the courts

The courts can initiate the settlement of routine claims before they are deeply mired in the litigation process. To a small degree this is being done now through settlement weeks and other marketing tactics as well as mandatory arbitration and mediation, but not on a consistent and effective basis. These procedures do not furnish settlement information, marketing and simply activity.

With evidence of the advantage of an early settlement to everyone involved, the courts could apply more pressure to have all parties buy into that settlement.

Negotiations enter the marketing age

Entering the information age assures that negotiators work from facts rather than the partially educated guess. By entering the marketing age and selling settlement with facts and benefits, negotiators and their clients would clearly come out ahead.

The goals set out early in this section can be achieved by using valid information to sell early settlements. Injured victims with legitimate negligence claims can receive equitable compensation without the cost and delay of litigation.

The goals set out early in this section can be achieved by using valid information to sell early settlements. Injured victims with legitimate negligence claims can receive equitable compensation without the cost and delay of litigation. Insurance carriers can save money by being cooperative and promptly compensating deserving claimants. Attorneys who represent claimants should receive reasonable compensation for services rendered. Defense attorneys should be able to market their litigation expertise for cases that warrant expertise.

These goals clearly translate into savings for the general population. Every time the insurance company saves money, it translates into policyholder savings. Every time a corporate defendant saves money, it translates into consumer savings. Every time the injured victim who deserves and receives their compensation early without bogging down the court system, taxpayers save money. These direct benefits mean policyholders, consumers and taxpayers need to fight the bad habits of negotiators. They need to help bring about change by selecting only insurance companies and lawyers who employ this more effective system of claim resolution.

#19

How To Take Control And Save Big

You are now aware that the $96 billion game is being played by many different players, which includes the policyholders, insurance companies, the self-insured, injured claimants, lawyers, regulators, judges and taxpayers. You may find yourself playing in more than one role.

You can take charge and achieve large savings at once. Each year you can achieve greater savings. I expect within five years the $96 billion game will be over. You will be able to save each year after that because you will no longer be playing a costly game.

The tort compensation system will be functioning efficiently with justice to all. The injured will promptly receive reasonable compensation for his injuries.

Personal injury litigation will only occur when the courts and juries have important questions to decide, such as serious questions of injury, fault and law, and to obtain information that can only be obtained through court proceedings.

Some suits will be filed because claimants sometimes hire an attorney when the statute of limitations is approaching its deadline that will bar a claim being made. Additional time may be needed to gather evidence and to negotiate a settlement.

Some suits may have to be filed for bargaining purposes. I estimate that only 20 percent of the present number of suits will be filed. Ten percent will be resolved within months upon the information secured.

Of the remaining ten percent, about two percent will be submitted to juries, and eight percent will go to arbitration, be tried by a judge, dismissed or withdrawn.

No longer will the courts be overburdened with litigation. Litigation will take months instead of years to resolve.

Based on the information in this book, more players will discover that they are playing a losing game and will take steps to end the losing game because it is in their best interest to do so. This makes your job easier. As knowledge gets around, fewer people will want to play this game and will take steps to get out.

Now, we will consider how you can take control with considerable savings and better justice to you.

You Can Take Control Now And Start Saving Big.

Since there are many different player groups, I will address each group individually, stating what each group can and should do to take control. I will address each player group in a separate chapter.

In the next chapter, we will tell the central character, the person or the company sued how they can take control.

#20

Sued: You Are The Central Character In The Game

As the central character in the 96 Billion Dollar Game, you are named in the complaint. It is also called a petition. You are sued and someone is claiming personal injury. They want money from you, most likely a lot of money. You may not be sued alone. It is now fashionable to sue everyone who has any possible connection with the cause of injury, though the connection may be remote or non-existent. You may be completely innocent of any blame yet, you may have to spend your time and money to attend legal proceedings.

Million of dollars may be demanded of you, including a request for punitive damages. It is fashionable to ask for a million dollars or more. You will discover by reading your insurance policy that you have no insurance coverage for punitive damage claims. Many states do not allow insurance protection for punitive damages because punitive damages are to punish you for conduct beyond ordinary carelessness.

To defend yourself effectively, your time, out-of-pocket expenses and attorney fees can mount up and can become sizable. Where punitive damages are sought, you have read that juries sometimes find against an innocent person or company for large sums. Worse yet, such debt is not dischargeable in bankruptcy.

You may be the sole person sued. You may find that you were sued even though your insurance carrier made a reasonable settlement offer. They may have offered more than a jury would likely award. You will quickly recognize you are playing the 96 Billion Dollar Game. In fact, you are a victim.

What can you do? You can check to be sure your insurance carrier has made a fair appraisal of the injury claim against you and if it has made an appropriate offer to settle. Your insurance carrier should show the claimant and claimant's attorney why it is in their best interest to settle promptly and dismiss the lawsuit.

You may have to retain an attorney to get this information. Some insurance companies will not furnish you with this information, though they should. Although, they have a fiduciary duty to you and have agreed to protect you, some insurance companies overlook keeping you informed. It's surprising this continues to happen since most insurance companies know that juries render verdicts in sizable amounts against insurance companies that don't treat their insureds right. Don't let them push you around. One reason they may refuse to give you this information is, they may be ashamed of their poor handling of your claim.

Under your insurance policy, you are assigned a defense counsel who is usually competent. Unfortunately, some companies continue to retain defense counsel who get poor results. This happens for many reasons. Friendship, years of representation, or they simply are not aware.

You may find it worthwhile to check out the track record of the counsel assigned to you. Your personal attorney may be able to give you a prompt answer. If he doesn't know, he can check.

Although, defense counsel may be highly competent,

they have an inherent conflict of interest problem. They may be more concerned with the insurance company's best interest, which may not be your best interest. The insurance company over the years may assign defense cases yielding defense counsel a lot of money. As the insured, you may be considered a minor client to the insurance company's defense attorney and they may never have to represent you again, but losing an important insurance client could be devastating to defense counsel.

Your defense counsel assigned under your insurance contract must represent you not the insurance company. Ask them to secure information about the probable verdict. If they don't, ask the insurance carrier to assign another counsel, one that is more interested in representing you.

If there is any question, retain counsel yourself to be sure you are being represented effectively and in your best interest. Your lawyer may make appropriate demands upon the defense counsel assigned and the carrier.

Unnecessary litigation can cost you time and money and may cost you more to purchase insurance. It may even put you in jeopardy when trying to obtain insurance from another carrier at reasonable rates.

Insurance companies are not likely to insure individuals and companies that are sued, especially repeatedly. This is true whether or not the suit or suits are the fault of your prior insurance carrier.

It is in your best interest to try to stay away from being insured by carriers that have not entered the information and marketing age. If you are insured with such a company, at your first opportunity, you should upon expiration of your coverage, get another carrier who will bring modern methods to handling your claims.

Refer to Chapter Three The Bankroll: $61 Billion in Policyholder Premiums and Cost and Chapter Four The Opening Bet: Insurers Gamble 40 Percent Of Your Premiums!

You do not want to play in the $96 billion game. You want to be treated in a business-like manner.

You may be sued over the limits of your insurance policy, however, a letter from your insurance company will inform you that you may wish to hire counsel to protect yourself from over the policy limit exposure.

Before spending money hiring counsel, ask your insurance carrier or the defense counsel to secure the information that I suggested earlier in this chapter. This refers to the insurance company obtaining information as to claim value and making an effective offer. If the carrier has not done so, it might be to your advantage to hire independent counsel. He will make the appropriate request from the insurance company.

Remember, defense counsel assigned to you has an obligation to represent your best interest. If you believe that assigned defense counsel is not representing you or conflicts of interest arise, make arrangements to be sure they do by securing legal counsel to represent you. Remember, if defense counsel fails to represent your best interest and you suffer a loss, they can be forced to respond to your loss. Juries are tough with defense counsel and insurance carriers that don't. Punitive damage awards can be in the millions. Good insurers and defense counsel know this and will be fair to you. It is in their best interest to do so, so give them a chance.

Ncxt, we examine how the policyholders can have a winning hand.

#21

Policyholders: The Winning Hand Can Be Yours

Now, you know how the 96 Billion Dollar Dame is played and few win. You, the policyholder can improve your hand and save thousands of dollars. You are also in a position as a player to stop this game that eats up your money.

You must realize that collectively with other policyholders, from insuring an old clunker, to insuring a fortune 500 corporation, you yield tremendous economic power, $124 billion each year and growing on automobile and casualty insurance.

You can change the game and end expensive and unnecessary litigation. This can translate into significant savings on your automobile and casualty insurance costs.

By helping to force insurance companies to stop needless litigation, you will save up to 35 percent of your insurance premium.

By avoiding or minimizing litigation, you will save considerable personal and business costs by not having to collect information, attend trial or hire attorneys to protect your interest in litigation.

By avoiding litigation, an individual or a family can save hundreds to thousands of dollars. A professional can save much more. A business can save many thousands of dollars.

We did not get into this game overnight and it will take years, probably five to end the 96 Billion Dollar Game. The big savings to you as a policyholder will be in ending the game. You will start to see additional savings in about a year as word gets around how wasteful and ridiculous the litigation game is.

In addition, you can make substantial premium savings right now. The reason is, insurance companies like other businesses vary drastically in overall efficiency. Some companies are more efficient than others in operating, marketing, selection of policyholders, handling their claims, and in generating and handling lawsuits. This results in different premium rates among companies.

The underlying philosophies of insurance companies vary widely. Sometimes an agent or underwriter will classify you in a higher rate class than another agent or underwriter at the same company for the same geographical area. Some insurance companies and their agents may want you as a policyholder more than others. For one month in your area or country wide, an insurance company may want more policyholders. The next month, they may restrict their writing of new insurance policies. They may only choose the best risks at the highest premium rates.

This means you have to compare rates. The large differences in rates may surprise you. See Appendix, page 265.

Automobile and Non-business Insurance

You may be able to save up to a thousand dollars a year or more on your automobile insurance premium right now and more over the years as the litigation in the pipeline dissipates.

For simple insurance policies like an automobile policy, the premiums charged by top rated companies for comparable policies differ a lot. Even in states where insurance companies rates are regulated, significant savings may be achieved and the winning hand can be yours by comparison shopping.

The Ohio Department of Insurance asked the largest 190 companies to quote prices they would charge specific drivers for the same coverage. As of September 1, 1991, they published their findings.

For example, age 22, single female, no driving age dependents for Cleveland. For one year, the premiums ranged from $709 to $5584.

For age 30, married couple, no driving age dependents the range was $567 to $3591. Two speeding tickets in the past year, the range was $586 to $3870.

For age 40, married couple, 17 year old daughter with driver training, the range was $752 to $6620.

I was informed that many other states, perhaps your own have made similar comparisons and they are available to you. Regardless, comparison shopping should yield you large savings.

To realize these substantial savings would only take about an hour or two of your time by simply placing a few phone calls to the agents of several insurance companies.

The details of this research can be found in the appendix.

BUSINESS RISKS

On business insurance, your savings can be in the thousands to the hundreds of thousands depending on the size of your business and your business insurance needs. For a small business, the savings can be thousands of dollars, a medium sized business could be in the tens or even hundreds of thousand of dollars and for the large corporation, the savings could be in the millions or even multi-millions.

Large companies today employ insurance managers, often called risk managers. They comparison shop for the most favorable insurance rates with the best coverage in a well rated company. Having a risk manager buy insurance can save a business considerable money on premiums. Business risks require special underwriters, people who consider the risk involved and determine what sort of premium should be charged to protect against such risk.

Insurance agents or brokers as in any other business, may or may not be competent or conscientious. They may represent or have access to very good companies or financially unstable companies that could become insolvent. A good agent may work with the best insurance companies available. Another agent may have companies that are rated financially lower or ones that don't offer the coverage or service of better rated insurance companies.

Why? Because some agents attract insureds but, due to their business or method of operation, generate few claims. These agents are attractive to insurance carriers. Naturally, the best insurance carriers will write policies for those companies that generate fewer costly problems and are more profitable. The less desirable business often goes to carriers that are less choosy. Of course, such companies want to attract the best business they can, but such companies may be risky for you.

Unfortunately, there's a built-in conflict of interest in the agent system. Agents are paid a percentage of the premium that they charge you. The higher the premium, the more they receive in commissions. The conscientious agent who shops around and get his client a good insurance carrier with lower rates will receive less in commissions than the less conscientious agent. Such an agent may not spend the time and effort to comparison shop. He may deliberately place his client with an insurance carrier that charges more to increase his commission.

For example, an agent that shops around may obtain comparable coverage in equally desirable companies one for a $10,000 annual premium and another for $14,000. This is not an unusual occurrence. At 20 percent, the difference to the agent is $1400 commission versus $1000. Commissions vary for different coverages and companies. Consider the difference, if the premium is for a larger business and the bids are $100,000 versus $140,000, the difference to the agent is $4,000. The good conscientious agent will attempt to place his client with the best companies at the lowest rates. However, the temptation is there to place you with the company with the highest premiums.

Fortunately, there are other people who are called risk management consultants who will work for you. Risk management consultants save their clients money in many different ways. Since they are paid directly by you, they will set up the insurance program to avoid over lapping risks. They will try to select the best company and obtain the best rates. They do not sell, but simply assist in the process.

The justification for having a risk management consultant is that he will provide you with the means to receive the best and fullest coverage at the lowest cost, saving you far more than the fees that they charge. You can locate one through the yellow pages, but be careful that you don't obtain an insurance agent that calls himself a risk manager. The reason is obvious, the insurance agent regardless of what he calls himself will still get paid by the insurance company. You want a risk manager who works only for you.

Although, the size of premiums is important, the business person must consider many other facts. Unlike auto insurance where there is a standard policy, the coverage and the needs of businesses vary widely. The premiums for similar coverage vary from company to company. Different insurance underwriters will look at your company's risk to their company's very differently. The policy coverage and restrictions may not be the same. The premiums that they demand may vary a lot.

The premiums charged by an insurance company is the financial stability of the company. Injury lawsuits against businesses can be for large amounts and may pend for years. Some claims may not surface until years and even decades later.

For example, many claims of injury due to asbestos exposure didn't surface until 20 years or more after the exposure. Since the injured person did not know that this would occur, the usual two year statute of limitations only applies when the injury has been discovered or should have been. It is important to have a financially secure insurance company as well as one that is expected to be in business many years from now. Unlike car insurance, if the insurance company fails, guaranty funds will pick up at least part of the loss. There may not be a guaranty fund for business coverage.

Some insurance companies, because of their claim

management policies or procedures, develop a lot of litigation while others develop very little. This should concern the person in charge of buying insurance. For a company whose insureds are sued often, this may require personnel to attend numerous legal processes and gather necessary but costly information. Frequently, one lawsuit can cost a business insured over $100,000 simply to service the lawsuit. Such service costs are not covered by the insurance contract.

The cost of lawsuits can be very expensive in other ways. In addition to the premium, lawsuits that should have been settled but were not, can cause injury to a company by unfavorable publicity. Needless lawsuits have injured businesses and caused the death of certain lines of products. For example, because of litigation without merit and the bad publicity, Audi's car sales dropped drastically. The car manufacturer lost hundreds of millions of dollars in sales.

An element of concern for the person responsible for buying business insurance is whether insurance companies overpay to settle their claims. Over payment of a few thousand dollars for each claim under circumstances where many claims without merit or much value surface, can quickly add up to over $50,000 to $100,000 when only 50 claims are involved. Where numerous claims are made, even a $100 over payment can become big money. A lawsuit involving a serious injury can be over paid by many thousands of dollars which results in increased insurance rates to you and the possible cancellation of the insurance policy. This could cause you some difficulty in obtaining reasonable rates elsewhere or coverage by another insurance company.

The business insurance buyer should find out what steps insurance companies are taking to reduce expensive litigation without overpaying injury claims with your insurance money. The buyer should select companies that handle their claims without developing unnecessary litigation.

Over payment and unnecessary litigation occur because of the outdated manner in which some insurance companies operate. Many do not make use of all the information and materials available to settle claims promptly for a reasonable cost without litigation. Some do, thus, it becomes very important for you to find out about the insurance company's claim policy. You may not find it desirable to keep switching companies. It is best to pick a company that handles their claims by using all of the information available to increase their efficiency and keep your premium as low as possible. Inquiry by you, your agent or risk manager can obtain this information. If they refuse to furnish such information, chances are that they will develop considerable litigation. Refusal can be a warning to seek another insurance company.

HELPING TO END THE 96 BILLION DOLLAR GAME

Now, you know that through comparison shopping you can achieve large and immediate savings. These, however, are only the initial dividends. Likewise for policy renewal.

Good comparison shopping will accomplish something much more important. It will force the poorly run insurance company to either go out of business or be forced to enter **The Information and Marketing Age.**

This will not only save you money, it also will make insurance companies give up your share of the 96 Billion Dollar Game. The savings will be important savings. Each year the amount can increase and be more significant. You, the policyholder has taken control. In a matter of five years or less, by doing some comparison shopping and saving money, you will help end your costly participation in the 96 Billion Dollar Game.

In the next chapter, we explore how insurance companies by entering the information and marketing age can save you money and at the same time become more profitable.

#22

Insurance Executives: You Can Deal Yourself A Winning Hand

In 1977, the All Industry Research Advisory Council (AIRAC) reported attorneys represented 31.3 percent of all automobile claimants. By 1987, the rate was up to 44.6 percent. In serious claims with economic loss, over 80 percent of the accident claimants hired attorneys. The rate goes up to 98.5 percent in commercial injury claims when the payout is expected to be more than $25,000 according to the Insurance Service Office (ISO).

Years ago, when I started to defend lawsuits for insurance companies, it was considered a serious black mark for an adjuster to "lose control" of a personal injury claim to an attorney. I had the impression that the percent of claims that went to attorney representatives was much, much less than it is now.

Do insurance officials, especially those in claims, ask themselves why the increase in attorney representation? I have no problem with attorneys representing the injured. The injured are entitled to be represented, if they wish. The large number that chose to be represented may indicate the insurance company's claim handling techniques are not as effective as they should be. This is especially true today when claim executives stress fairness in the settlement of claims.

More questions must be raised when AIRAC reported that 18.1 percent of all auto claims and ISO 25.7 percent of all commercial injury claims resulted in litigation. A large percentage of personal injury claims end up in a lawsuit. Why so many? Obviously, there must be serious deficiencies in dealing effectively with attorneys.

The most important question raised is why so many claims are allowed to enter litigation?

Eventually, 90 percent of personal injury cases in litigation settle without trial.

Of course, any insurance claim executive can cite many reasons for it happening, while exonerating himself of all blame. But, are they valid? You should realize the insurance company holds some very important cards actually the most crucial, the Purse.

Why are insurance companies allowing costly litigation to develop and last for a long time? The answer is that most of them have not entered the information and marketing age in the handling of their claims.

Although, insurance companies operate in the jury system, and juries are the main arbitrators of value, it is still baffling that so few bother to get information available from several sources on what juries do in personal injury cases. You can find pertinent information compiled into statistical tables. These furnish the probability of winning an award in the various liability situations and awards for the various injuries.

Why so many insurance companies still operate in the valuation of their personal injury claims using the partially educated guess rather than real information based upon actual verdicts is hard to understand. It's like playing stud poker without bothering to know your hole card. Is your company using the partially educated guess in evaluating your claims?

In fact, many claims people operate on information that they glean from newspaper accounts and scuttlebutt. Unfortunately, these are usually news about very large verdicts that give insurance executives the impression that juries are giving away their money. The result, often the evaluation by the insurance company is far higher than juries can be expected to award. As a result, payments to settle claims and lawsuits are too often far beyond reality.

How do your settlements measure up? Have you checked lately?

Everyone is interested in "What's in it for me"? "What's best for me"? The insurance representative will simply dangle more and more money, hoping the injured claimant will finally say, "yes." If the amount offered is often far more than a jury would likely award, this means the offer is too high. This also creates a problem with the lawyer who later enters the case. Should the company offer even more, though it has already offered more than the case is worth?

Can the insurance company expect the lawyer to settle for the same amount as previously offered? Even some "sweetening up" will rarely help. The attorney has to be paid. He has to get more for his client and not a few dollars, but enough to justify hiring the lawyer.

Remember, the lawyer probably told the claimant when he or she was considering hiring him "their offer is too low, I will get you a lot more". Actually, this statement will be frequently made even if the lawyer doesn't know enough about the facts or the case value to make such a promise.

In later contacts with the lawyer, including the pre-trial and the trial room, the negotiations may center on increasing the offer, regardless of its real value, based upon what a jury would likely do.

The result, the case continues increasing the cost of litigation. The offers continues to inch upwards until the case is settled either in the trial room or is tried to a verdict.

There is some pertinent information that the insurance company could and should have obtained and used.

The insurance carrier should find out what the jury is likely to award. Refer to charts L and M. It should then determine the settlement value. The amount a jury is likely to award and the settlement value are different.

To arrive at a jury verdict requires litigation expenses and these expenses must be deducted from the likely award. In addition, the probability of a defense verdict also must be considered.

For example, in an injury case (illustrated in charts L and M) where the probable verdict is $50,000 and the probability of a verdict for the injured is 57 percent and the estimated litigation expenses to a verdict is $7,934.

Probable Verdict Amount	$50,000
Plaintiff Litigation Costs	7,934
Net Value At Verdict	42,066
Probability Of Verdict	
	x57%
Basic Settlement Value	$23,978

To bring the case to a verdict, a lawyer to represent the injured must be hired. Let us assume (as in chart N) a 33 1/3% fee, a common contingent fee basis. The settlement value is decreased by the attorney fee. The injured would realize $17,305.

CHART L

CASE DESCRIPTION
Doe vs. Roe

INCIDENT DATE
October 6, 1985

INCIDENT
Two vehicle collision at a 4-way intersection controlled by stop signs in all four directions. Each driver contends that the other failed to stop and failed to yield the right-of-way. Police responded to the scene of the accident and neither driver was cited.

COUNSEL
John Q. Attorney, Esquire
444 Main Street
Cleveland, Ohio 44115
(216) 444-4444

SPECIALS

To-Date	Medical	$4,000
	Wage Loss	$800
Non-	Medical	$0
Recoverable	Wage Loss	$0

Evaluator	Don Marshall, Ph.D.
Date	August 13, 1989

Disposition	Undetermined
Amount	$0

CHART M

	Recovery	**Injury**
Liability		
INTERSECTION, 2-Way or 4-Way Stop		
Basic Injury Value:		$36,480
VERTEBRA, Fracture		
CASE-SPECIFIC ADJUSTMENTS:	0%	
Impairment, Permanent, Pain & Weakness		
Injury Challenged by Defense,	0%	3%
Permanent Impairment Contested	0%	(8%)
Plaintiff Sex & Age at Incident, Female	0%	
30-39	0%	10%
State & County Venue, Ohio, Cuyahoga	0%	5%
Witnesses, Medical: (Contested Injury Only), Plaintiff & Defendant	0%	23%
Total Adjustments to Injury Value		33%
Total Injury Value		$48,518
Adjustment for Non Recoverable Specials		0
Adjusted Total Injury Value		$48,518
PROBABLE VERDICT AMOUNT		33%
		$50,000
Basic Recovery Rate	57%	
Total Adjustments to Recovery Rate	x 0%	
PROBABILITY OF PLAINTIFF VERDICT	57%	
ACTUARIAL VERDICT VALUE		$28,500

CHART N

NET FEE TO ATTORNEY FOR INJURED PERSON

AT SETTLEMENT PRIOR TO SUIT		
Probable Verdict Amount	15%	$50,000
Plaintiff Total Litigation Cost		(7,934)
Net Value at Plaintiff Verdict		42,066
Probability of Plaintiff Verdict		57%
BASIC SETTLEMENT VALUE		$23,978
Out-of-Pocket Costs Prior to Suit	1%	(637)
NET VALUE AT SETTLEMENT		$23,341
AT POINT OF VERDICT		
Probable Verdict Amount		$50,000
Out-of-Pocket Costs	9%	(4,686)
Net Value at Plaintiff Verdict		45,314
Probability of Plaintiff Verdict		57%
Net Value		25,829
AT PLAINTIFF VERDICT		$50,000
Probable Verdict Amount	9%	(4,686)
Out-of-Pocket Costs		45,314
Net Value		
ATTORNEY FEE %	33%	
NET VALUE AT SETTLEMENT		$23,341
Attorney's Fee		7,702
Time & Costs Prior to Suit	2%	(1,160)
Net Fee		6,542
NET VALUE AT POINT OF VERDICT		25,829
Attorney's Fee		8,524
Litigation Time & Costs	15%	(7,926)
Net Fee		598
NET VALUE AT PLAINTIFF VERDICT		45,314
Attorney's Fee		14,954
Litigation Time & Costs	15%	(7,926)
Net Fee		7,028
NET LOSS AT DEFENSE VERDICT		($12,612)

CHART N COMPARISON: FEE TO ATTORNEY FOR INJURED PERSON NET FEE AT SETTLEMENT & VERDICT

Net Year	Future Value 8.3750% $ 6,542	POINT OF VERDICT Present Value (9.2530%) $ 598	PLAINTIFF VERDICT Present Value (9.2530%) $ 7,028	DEFENSE VERDICT Annual Increase 9.3600% ($ 12,612)
1	7,090	542	6,377	(13,792)
2	7,684	492	5,787	(15,083)
3	8,328	447	5,252	(16,495)
4	9,025	405	4,766	(18,039)
5	9,781	368	4,325	(19,728)
6	10,600	334	3,925	(21,574)
7	11,488	303	3,562	(23,594)
8	12,450	275	3,232	(25,802)
9	13,493	249	2,933	(28,217)

In addition, personal litigation costs must be considered. What would happen if the case is tried and a jury awarded the injured the probable verdict amount $50,000 or nothing?

This information can be quickly calculated by a computer and the printout would be as follows (see comparison set in bottom third of charts N, O and P).

It takes time to go from filing a lawsuit to the courtroom for a trial. If the claimant waits until their case goes to trial and post trial procedures, they cannot spend any money until he receives a favorable verdict and is paid. Comparisons must be made for the time in litigation with the proposed settlement offer drawing interest in a bank and the effect of inflation, etc. The bottom portions of charts: N, O and P comparison shows this for one to nine years.

The first column Chart P is for settlement. It is assumed that settlement is or can be arranged within a reasonable time and without litigation.

Future Value is based upon the settlement earning interest. The illustrated chart uses 8.370 percent based upon 30 year U.S. Government Bonds. Interest rates that can be earned fluctuate. Economists use the 30 year bond as the benchmark. Shorter term bonds, C.D.'s and Bank Deposits fluctuate too much. When this table was calculated, the interest rate was 8.3750 percent. As I write this book, it is about two points lower.

A year from now the future value interest rate may be higher or lower than we are using. The purpose is to illustrate that money earning interest increases. In our example, the $17,983 net settlement in three years average litigation time in many cities becomes $22,890.

CHART O
NET SHARE TO INJURED PERSON REPRESENTED BY COUNSEL

AT SETTLEMENT PRIOR TO SUIT		
Probable Verdict Amount	15%	$50,000
		(7,934)
		42,066
Plaintiff Total Litigation Cost		57%
Net Value at Plaintiff Verdict		
Probability of Plaintiff Verdict		$23,978
	1%	(637)
BASIC SETTLEMENT VALUE		
Out-of-Pocket Costs Prior to Suit		$23,341
NET VALUE AT SETTLEMENT		
		$50,000
AT POINT OF VERDICT	9%	(4,686)
Probable Verdict Amount		45,314
Out-of-Pocket Costs		57%
Net Value at Plaintiff Verdict		25,829
Probability of Plaintiff Verdict		
Net Value		$50,000
	9%	(4,686)
AT PLAINTIFF VERDICT		45,314
Probable Verdict Amount		
Out-of-Pocket Costs		
Net Value	67%	
PLAINTIFF SHARE %		$23,341
		15,638
NET VALUE AT SETTLEMENT	1%	(100)
Plaintiff Share		15,538
Personal Costs		
Net Share		$25,829
		17,305
NET VALUE AT POINT OF VERDICT	1%	(526)
Plaintiff Share		16,779
Personal Costs		
Net Share		$45,314
		30,360
NET VALUE AT PLAINTIFF VERDICT	1%	(526)
Plaintiff Share		29,834
Personal Costs		
Net Share		($526)
NET LOSS AT DEFENSE VERDICT		

CHART O COMPARISON: NET SHARE TO INJURED PERSON REPRESENTED BY COUNSEL

NET SHARE AT SETTLEMENT & VERDICT

Net Year	Future Value 8.3750% $15,538	POINT OF VERDICT Present Value (6.3600%) $16,779	PLAINTIFF VERDICT Present Value (6.3600%) $29,834	DEFENSE VERDICT Annual Increase 9.3600% (526)
1	16,840	15,712	27,937	(575)
2	18,250	14,713	26,160	(629)
3	19,778	13,777	24,496	(688)
4	21,435	12,901	22,938	(752)
5	23,230	12,080	21,479	(823)
6	25,175	11,312	20,113	(900)
7	27,284	10,593	18,834	(984)
8	29,569	9,919	17,636	(1,076)
9	32,045	9,288	16,515	(1,177)

CHART P

NET SHARE TO INJURED PERSON REPRESENTED BY COUNSEL

AT SETTLEMENT PRIOR TO SUIT		
Probable Verdict Amount		$50,000
Plaintiff Total Litigation Cost	15%	(7,934)
Net Value at Plaintiff Verdict		42,066
Probability of Plaintiff Verdict		57%
BASIC SETTLEMENT VALUE		$23,978
Adjustment for Direct Settlement	25%	(5,994)
NET VALUE AT SETTLEMENT		$17,983
AT POINT OF VERDICT		
Probable Verdict Amount		$50,000
Out-of-Pocket Costs	9%	(4,686)
Net Value at Plaintiff Verdict		45,314
Probability of Plaintiff Verdict		57%
Net Value		25,829
AT PLAINTIFF VERDICT		
Probable Verdict Amount		$50,000
Out-of-Pocket Costs	9%	(4,686)
Net Value		45,314
NET VALUE AT SETTLEMENT		$17,983
Plaintiff Share		17,983
Net Share		17,983
NET VALUE AT POINT OF VERDICT		$25,829
Plaintiff Share		17,305
Personal Costs	1%	(526)
Net Share		16,779
NET VALUE AT PLAINTIFF VERDICT		$45,314
Plaintiff Share		30,360
Personal Costs	1%	(526)
Net Share		29,834
NET LOSS AT DEFENSE VERDICT		

CHART P COMPARISON: NET SHARE AT SETTLEMENT & VERDICT

Net Year	Future Value 8.3750% $17,983	POINT OF VERDICT Present Value (6.3600%) $16,779	PLAINTIFF VERDICT Present Value (6.3600%) $29,834	DEFENSE VERDICT Annual Increase 9.3600% ($526)
1	19,840	15,712	27,937	(575)
2	21,122	14,713	26,160	(629)
3	22,890	13,777	24,496	(688)
4	24,808	12,901	22,938	(752)
5	26,885	12,080	21,479	(823)
6	29,137	11,312	20,113	(900)
7	31,557	10,593	18,834	(984)
8	34,222	9,919	17,636	(1,076)
9	37,088	9,288	16,515	(1,177)

Point of Verdict, the second column illustrates the present value of a verdict. This considers loss of investment potential, inflation, and increase in verdict size over time as the litigated case pends in court. We used five percent as the inflation rate, which decreased the purchasing power of the money. Over time, due to increased medical costs etc., jurors bring in larger verdicts. Jury Verdict Research found that the verdict increased annually by 7.22 percent. The cumulative effect of the loss of investment potential, inflation and increase in verdict size is -6.36 percent. That is the money received by a verdict because of the time required in litigation, decreases in value and it buys less. Note that the $16,779 net in three years becomes $13,779.

The third column assumes that the injured person won the full amount. Note that in three years the $29,834 net decreases to $24,496, and in four years it is worth less than the settlement. The injured didn't take the 43 percent chance of a defense verdict and thus getting nothing.

Chart N shows how litigation affects the attorney representing the injured.

Chart O shows how litigation affects the injured represented by counsel.

The insurance company should also know how litigation affects them. See charts Q, R,S and T.

When an insurance company settles a case, there are no further expenses. However, if it litigates, its expenses increase. Verdicts go up and inflation increase the cost of services, overhead and personnel, as well as lost interest on money used to pay expenses. In addition, the insurance company incurs additional defense fees and expenses. This is offset only partially by the interest it earns on the money it is holding to pay the judgement.

CHART Q

DEFENSE COSTS: INJURED PERSON REPRESENTED BY COUNSEL

AT SETTLEMENT PRIOR TO SUIT		
Probable Verdict Amount		($50,000)
Plaintiff Total Litigation Cost	15%	7,934
Net Value at Plaintiff Verdict		($42,066)
Probability of Plaintiff Verdict		57%
BASIC SETTLEMENT VALUE		($23,978)
Out-of-Pocket Costs Prior to Suit	0%	0
Total Cost		($23,341)
AT POINT OF VERDICT		
Probable Verdict Amount		($50,000)
Defense Costs	29%	(14,742)
Cost at Plaintiff Verdict		(64,752)
Probability of Plaintiff Verdict		57%
Total Cost		($36,903)
AT PLAINTIFF VERDICT		
Probable Verdict Amount		($50,000)
Defense Cost	29%	(14,742)
Total Cost		(64,742)
AT DEFENSE VERDICT		
Defense Cost	29%	($14,742)

CHART R

COMPARISON: NET COST AT SETTLEMENT & VERDICT

Net Year	Settlement $23,978	POINT OF VERDICT Annual Increase (11.7200%) $36,903	PLAINTIFF VERDICT Annual Increase (11.7200%) $50,000	DEFENSE VERDICT Annual Increase 9.3600% 14,742
1		41,223	64,742	16,122
2		46,060	71,982	17,631
3		51,458	80,038	19,281
4		57,489	89,002	21,086
5		64,227	98,978	23,059
6		71,754	110,080	25,218
7		80,164	122,438	27,578
8		89,559	136,192	30,160
9		100,055	156,504	32,982

CHART S

DEFENSE COSTS AT DIRECT SETTLEMENT WITH INJURED PERSON

AT SETTLEMENT PRIOR TO SUIT		
Probable Verdict Amount		($50,000)
Plaintiff Total Litigation Cost	15%	7,934
Net Value at Plaintiff Verdict		($42,066)
Probability of Plaintiff Verdict		57%
BASIC SETTLEMENT VALUE		($23,978)
Adjustment for Direct Settlement:	25%	5,994
Total Cost		($17,983)
AT POINT OF VERDICT		
Probable Verdict Amount		($50,000)
Defense Costs	29%	(14,742)
Cost at Plaintiff Verdict		(64,752)
Probability of Plaintiff Verdict		57%
Total Cost		($36,903)
AT PLAINTIFF VERDICT		
Probable Verdict Amount		($50,000)
Defense Cost	29%	(14,742)
Total Cost		(64,742)
AT DEFENSE VERDICT		
Defense Cost	29%	($14,742)

CHART T

COMPARISON: NET COST AT SETTLEMENT & VERDICT

Net Year	Settlement $23,978	POINT OF VERDICT Annual Increase (11.7200%) $36,903	PLAINTIFF VERDICT Annual Increase (11.7200%) $50,000	DEFENSE VERDICT Annual Increase 9.3600% 14,742
1		41,223	72,330	16,122
2		46,060	80,807	17,631
3		51,458	90,277	19,281
4		57,489	100,858	21,086
5		64,227	112,678	23,059
6		71,754	125,884	25,218
7		80,164	140,638	27,578
8		89,559	157,121	30,160
9		100,055	175,535	32,982
				Plus Defense Cost Increase

The cumulative effect expenses increased at 11.72 percent.

Chart Q and S sets out the figures and defense costs at direct settlement. Chart R sets out costs where an attorney represents the injured in litigation.

Note, that in three years, the $23,975 proposed settlement becomes $51,458 at point of verdict. If the insurance company loses, the cost goes to $90,277. If the insurance company wins, the cost is $19,281 to them.

One additional piece of information should be obtained if possible, and that is, the expected time from filing to verdict. Based on this, the insurance company can structure its settlement offer (see chart T). For example, if the average time from filing to verdict is three years, the adjuster will be prepared to show the financial effect of that delay. Since time to verdict may vary, the adjuster should be prepared to show the financial effect.

Now, the adjuster is ready to approach the injured. Does the insurance company provide their adjusters with this important information? Being in the information age, the adjuster should be prepared to market the settlement.

With this knowledge, as an injured claimant, you could make a rational choice. This information can be printed out showing it came from an impartial source. The insurance company, depending upon the situation and its policy, makes a reasonable offer to the claimant. The injured is shown what's in it for him under several different situations. The injured can accept the offer or make a counter offer. The insurance company may wish to accept.

EXHIBIT B
TIME SPAN BETWEEN INCIDENT DATE AND TRIAL DATE BY COUNTY

County		Average: Year(s)	Month(s)	Median: Year(s)	Month(s)	Mode: Year(s)	Month(s)	Minimum: Year(s)	Month(s)	Maximum: Year(s)	Month(s)
Baltimore	MD	2	11	2	7	2	0	0	5	7	3
Bexar (San Antonio)	TX	2	8	2	3	---	---	1	1	6	11
Bronx	NY	4	8	3	11	2	6	0	11	13	5
Broward (Ft. Lauderdale)	FL	3	6	3	3	3	8	0	9	7	9
Cook (Chicago)	IL	6	2	5	10	2	7	0	4	16	2
Cuyahoga (Cleveland)	OH	3	3	2	11	2	6	1	4	12	5
Dallas	TX	3	6	3	5	2	11	0	8	7	3
Denver	CO	3	1	3	0	2	10	0	11	9	6
Fulton (Atlanta)	GA	3	4	3	0	2	9	1	0	7	9
Harris (Houston)	TX	3	10	3	3	2	8	2	1	6	3
Hennepin (Minneapolis)	MN	4	1	4	0	4	0	2	8	6	1
King (Seattle)	WA	3	11	3	8	2	11	1	1	15	8
Los Angeles	CA	5	0	5	6	6	0	0	9	14	1
Multnomah (Portland)	OR	2	11	2	10	2	8	0	11	12	1
New York	NY	5	5	4	9	3	11	1	3	15	5
Palm Beach	FL	3	3	2	10	2	1	0	10	8	10
Philadelphia	PA	6	1	6	0	10	5	0	7	12	9
Queens	NY	5	0	4	4	3	8	0	11	10	9
San Diego	CA	4	1	3	9	2	5	1	5	10	9
San Francisco	CA	3	11	3	6	2	3	0	6	14	5
St. Louis	MO	3	11	3	8	3	4	1	5	8	1
Suffolk (Boston)	MA	5	11	6	5	2	1	0	8	9	10
Wayne (Detroit)	MI	4	4	3	11	3	11	2	0	10	8
West Palm Beach	FL	3	4	3	7	1	9	1	9	5	2

Let us assume that the claimant fails to settle and consults and attorney before the adjuster can make an offer to the injured. The adjuster is then able to make an offer to the injured's lawyer supported by impartial information.

The attorney can see what's in it for his client and for him and can make a counter offer that may be accepted. The attorney can make an informed recommendation to his client based upon reliable information.

Assume the attorney is considering litigation, the information furnished will show whether the offer by the insurance company is fair.

If the offer is fair and the attorney advises his client contrary to the information and the odds, and if the claimant later receives less money by verdict or settlement including the effect of interest that could have been earned, the attorney exposes himself to a valid legal malpractice claim.

If your adjuster uses this information along with marketing, most cases would settle promptly and without litigation. Is your company using marketing techniques to settle your claims or simply throwing money at claimants and their lawyers?

We have looked at the positive side of taking control. Let us consider an equally important reason you must start using information and marketing in the management of your claims.

Bad faith is a growing and serious problem for the insurance companies. In Chapter Four, <u>The Opening Bet: Insurers Gamble 40 Percent Of Your Premiums</u>, you will notice the large punitive awards that juries are awarding in bad faith claims.

Insurance companies jolted with multi-million dollar verdicts are discovering that failure to honor a demand within policy limits or to be greeted by a verdict over policy limits can be very costly. This is especially true when actuarial information would have shown that a verdict over-the-limits was likely or that the offer was reasonable and should have been accepted. And that the insurance company was not aware of the probabilities is not a defense.

You have to be prepared to show you relied upon competent information when structuring your offers and your refusals of demands.

In suits over-the-limits, a simple letter advising the insured to consider obtaining his own counsel will not necessarily be sufficient to protect you. This may be especially true where the insured does not retain over-the-limits counsel. **You will have to give your insured directly or through defense counsel assigned to him, verdict information so he can make an informed decision.** In addition, he should be kept informed as to any demands and offers made.

You are also discovering the legal duties you may have to the claimant other than a fair offer. You have to provide sufficient and competent information so the claimant can make an informed decision.

Overpaying claims to avoid litigation and generating avoidable litigation are costly to the insurance carrier. This practice can result in the loss of important commercial accounts. Some large insurers faced with increased premiums are transferring to more efficiently operated insurance companies, others are switching to insurance alternatives such as self-insurance, captive insurance companies and risk retention groups. Insurance companies that incur the expense of avoidable litigation or overpay claims make themselves non-competitive.

The most important social force you face, especially if you are an automobile insurer, is the public revolt against high premiums. Rollbacks in premiums of companies that are already losing money can force such companies to re-evaluate their valuation and handling of personal injury claims and lawsuits. Likewise, the reluctance of insurance commissioners to grant rate increases routinely is forcing insurance companies to re-evaluate their handling of claims.

As you are aware, some insurance commissioners, California's for example are looking at the soundness of insurance company operations.

The insurance company, by decreasing litigation expenses, avoiding needless overpayment and bad faith claims, can save their insurers almost 35 percent in premium costs. By doing this, the insurance company can operate profitably.

In the Appendix, I recommend several books that you will find invaluable in helping you to manage your claims.

In the next chapter, we consider what the self-insured should do.

#23

The Self Insured: You Are A Major Player

You are a major player. The game is costing you $18 billion! Look at Chapter Nine, The Side Bet: Self Insurer $18 Billion.

In many respects, you should do what is recommended for insurance companies, as your problems are much the same. You are playing the game with your dollars not those of the policyholder and you have to be more careful with them.

You have to enter the information and marketing age. If you use an independent adjustment firm, be sure their investigators and adjusters use information and marketing when they are trying to settle your claims.

In the next chapter, we discuss how the injured can keep from being a victim again.

#24

The Injured: To Keep From Being A Victim Again, Keep Your Eye On The Pot

The game is about you. You are playing the leading role. Most of the pot is to compensate you for your injury and unless you keep your eye on the pot, it may disappear in part or all.

If you are hurt due to someone else's fault, that person may have to compensate you for your injuries. The purpose is as completely as possible to make you whole again.

Since the responsible person or entity cannot cure you, especially if you suffered a serious, permanent, disabling injury, they must respond with a substitute, money. If you cannot agree on how much, a jury will decide for you. That doesn't mean that all personal injury claims have to be submitted to a jury.

Juries follow patterns in their monetary awards for similar injuries with similar economic loss. These patterns can be predicted with reasonable probability. Juries also follow predictable patterns when deciding fault (liability for or against the plaintiff) in similar types of cases. In the past 25 years, juries have found for the injured 60 to 63 percent of the time and 75 to 78 percent of the time in rear-end cases.

For over 30 years, actuarial tables of injury values and verdict outcomes have been available. They are used by many attorneys representing the injured as well as the defense, insurance company claim personnel, governments and self-insurers.

Surprisingly, many attorneys with little or no jury experience prefer to guess at what a jury will likely award, which is often far from reality. Some insurance companies with limited trial experience do the same. The result is often inequitable settlements and more litigation. Litigation only serves to delay often for years fair compensation to the injured. Worse yet, as a result of the delay, the injured often receives much less than he should have. This is due to lost interest, increased expenses and a loss of purchasing power due to inflation.

The injured is often counseled by lawyers who use the partially educated guess to turn down offers often of large amounts only to be awarded nothing. You have been victimized again.

You can honestly be called a victim if you are hurt because of someone else's fault. To prevent being victimized again you must insist upon certain information. If you are dealing with an adjuster for the insurance company or self-insurer, you must request that you be furnished in writing with up-to-date impartial information. This information is readily available and should tell you your chances of winning and what you can expect a jury to award you. You also should ask for an estimate of how much litigation will cost you and how long before your case reach the trial room. You need this information to make an intelligent, informed decision.

If the offer by the insurance company doesn't compare favorably with this information, or if the adjuster refuses or fails to furnish it, you may need to hire an attorney.

When you hire an attorney, make sure that the attorney is competent in personal injury cases. The attorney you hire should agree to furnish you the information requested from the insurance adjuster.

Many attorneys prefer to let litigation make up for their lack of knowledge regarding your claim's worth. Litigation also may be an indication of their lack of negotiation ability. This robs you of a prompt settlement and you will most likely pay dearly. Keep your eye on the pot!

Read Chapter Six, Victim Again: The Injured Lose $9 Billion.

Refer also to the Appendix for information about a book that will help you deal with the insurance adjuster and help you in hiring and using an attorney.

In the next chapter, we examine how the lawyer can win a bigger pot for his client and for himself.

#25

Lawyer (For The Injured) You Can Win A Bigger Pot For Your Client And Yourself

Over the years, I have been impressed at how dedicated plaintiff attorneys are to your clients. You work long hours over months and years to discover evidence, law and techniques that lead to highly favorable settlements and verdicts for your clients. Because of your success, you are criticized by insurance companies, defense lawyers and business people as though you are a highway robber. Actually, you are often a victim of your own zeal! Your client also is often a victim.

Without realizing you are playing in the $96 billion game and losing, it is costing you and your client. You are often using litigation as a substitute for evaluating and negotiating your cases. This is expensive and time consuming. You can accomplish better results quicker and at less cost. Your client can get settlements in a few months instead of years. The net will be larger. Your clients will have money to spend. They can earn interest on the rest.

The proof is set out in Chapter Six, Victim Again: The Injured Lose $9 Billion. And you too will realize more money with less work.

Why work hard over years only to decrease your income? See Chapter Seven, Raising The Bet: Plaintiff Attorneys Risk $7.5 Billion.

There are other reasons to use information instead of litigation. Litigation through trial is seldom profitable to the attorney. Worse yet, 37 to 40 percent of the injured receive nothing due to defense verdicts. You not only lost the time you spent, but all the expenses you advanced as well. What's even worse, you may have recommended that a sizable offer be declined. If you had checked jury verdict probability tables, you would have realized that the offer may have been reasonable and should have been accepted.

In malpractice claims against doctors, a lack of informed consent is often the basis. Do you think lawyers are immune from the requirement of informed consent? Since information from competent, impartial sources about the chance of a favorable verdict is available, did you use this information in informing your client of his chances of a favorable verdict? Do you think that the partially educated guess is a good defense, when better information was available?

How about a client discovering that he waited years to get less purchasing power than an offer prior to litigation? That he lost interest he could have earned? We are in the information age. Clients are better informed. They do not hesitate to sue their lawyers when they find they have not been properly represented.

In the many personal injury cases in which I have taken depositions of the injured, I was surprised that so few were represented by the attorney who represented them for a previous injury. Although, the question was not pertinent to the lawsuit, I always asked why new counsel? The claimant's new attorney was just as interested in the answer as I. The answer frequently was dissatisfaction with the previous lawyer or firm.

This dissatisfaction centered on the belief that the

attorney got a poor settlement or verdict for the client. This was true even when the nature of the accident and injury clearly indicated that the lawyer delivered a very good result. After reading and hearing of large verdicts, some client's believe the smaller settlements are a result of poor legal representation. Would the client relationship be better if the lawyer furnished impartial information showing how good the settlement really was?

The long delay also was mentioned with the belief that a good lawyer would have secured a settlement much quicker.

You will serve your clients and yourself better by not playing this 96 Billion Dollar Game.

#26

The Defense Attorney: You Can Help Reduce The Pot

You play a very important role in the game. You also can play a leading role in ending the game. However, you need the cooperation of the insurance carrier and the self-insured to support you in litigation and negotiating settlements.

They can authorize you to secure the tools you need. I am referring to the actuarial verdict information available as well as verdicts in similar cases.

Many companies do not permit defense counsel to negotiate settlements in personal injury litigation cases. This may be a serious mistake. As active defense counsel in your area, you know the injured's attorney better than the insurance adjuster. More important, the plaintiff attorney has more respect for you. You also have effective tools you can use to assist toward a reasonable settlement such as motions, depositions, and your effective trial ability.

More insurance companies and self-insurers should realize they need attorneys to represent them in affecting equitable settlements with a minimum of litigation.

There will always be cases because of questions of law, liability, or injury that must go to trial. There will also be cases which require litigation to determine the facts necessary to discover whether the carrier owes anything and if so, how much? Once these questions have been resolved it is important for the defense lawyer to become an efficient negotiator and assist towards a prompt and equitable settlement.

The problem is effective negotiation and the necessary preparation takes time. Some insurance companies balk at paying for it. For example, an insurance company once assigned me its first case. Their insurance agent recommended me and an important insured was worried.

It was a lawsuit involving a pedestrian claiming she was crossing in a crosswalk, in a heavy rain storm, to catch a bus and was struck by the insured. She suffered very serious and permanent injuries. The insurance company was worried about over-the-limit exposure. They gave me settlement authority up to policy limits which were substantial with instructions to use all if necessary, to get a prompt settlement.

The insured never saw the pedestrian until after he had hit her 30 feet beyond the crosswalk. I visited the accident scene and noticed that the only shelter from the rain an entrance to a store was 30 feet from the crosswalk, directly across the street from the bus stop. There was no shelter at the bus stop. A bend in the street prevented a person in the store entrance from seeing a bus until it arrived at the bus stop. The pedestrian must have sheltered herself from the rain. When the bus arrived at the bus stop, obviously she must have run to catch the bus. Most likely, she did not see our insured's car and the insured did not see her because of the heavy downpour.

I ordered a prompt deposition of the women. Since she could not leave the house because of her injuries, I went to her home. She readily admitted getting out of the rain by standing in the store's entrance. She also admitted crossing directly across the street when her bus arrived.

I took her attorney to the site, and showed him that his client crossed 30 feet from the crosswalk. A reasonable settlement was quickly worked out at only a fraction of the policy limits. His client would not agree. The attorney asked me to assist him by explaining why she should accept the settlement. I went to his client's home and assisted him. When I phoned for a settlement check, the Vice President of Claims could not believe the case was settled so quickly and for much less under the policy limits.

But, when I sent my bill, a very small fraction of the amount saved for my time, which was an accurate account, the company said they never paid so much for defense services in a case where no answer had been filed and was less than a month in a lawyer's office. The company never sent me another case.

Some companies, however, would send me cases already in litigation sometimes over a hundred in a group, including cases from other states because of my reputation for getting prompt, reasonable settlements. May be because I was the author of "Better Settlements Through Leverage." They continued to send me cases until I retired from the practice of law.

Many defense attorneys have reported to me similar dissatisfied billing experiences. As a result, they would avoid spending time negotiating. If they were authorized more money, they simply conveyed the information. No attempt was made to explain or persuade the plaintiff attorney why the increased offer should be accepted.

Insurance companies must recognize that effective negotiation often takes more time than legal processes, such as preparing an answer to the petition, motions and even some depositions. Legal processes are seldom questioned in billing.

I recognize some defense attorneys are poor negotiators. Whatever authority they are given, they simply convey to the plaintiff attorney. Today's defense firms usually have defense attorneys of many different skills. Effective negotiators should be included. If the defense firm does not have any attorney with such qualifications, another firm may be sought.

Defense counsel has a serious conflict of interest that can occur. The insurance carrier assigns the defense cases to their defense counsel. Often, the number are many and the billings are large. To keep them coming, the insurance company's personnel must be kept happy. Unfortunately, too often the best interest of the insured and the insurance company differs.

Where there is a conflict of interest, defense counsel owe their primary duty to the insured they are defending. Some defense counsel avoid recognizing the conflict of interest, thereby conducting the defense which may not be in the best interest of the insured.

For example, in an over-the-limits lawsuit, a letter is sent to the insured informing him that he may wish to hire an attorney to represent him on his over-the-limit exposure. Frequently, the insured does not hire an attorney to represent him in the over-the-limits exposure. Word often gets around that a personal attorney is not needed. This could be from past lawsuits, advice of a friend, or hints by the insurance agent that hiring an attorney is an unnecessary expense.

The defense attorney does not bother to get information that shows that an over-the-limit judgement is probable. However, he is aware of this but does not alert the insured to this probability. The verdict is over-the-limits. The insured's home or business is in jeopardy as the injured wants to collect the entire judgement. The insured may sue defense counsel for bad faith and or malpractice and the insurance carrier for bad faith. It is clear that today, if defense counsel does not alert the insured he is defending of the probability of an over-the-limit verdict, he may find himself facing a malpractice claim. Even worse, it may include a count for punitive damages. Verdicts in such cases can run in to the millions.

The future of defense attorneys lies in the handling of complex cases that the insurance companies staff trial attorneys cannot effectively handle. This will allow defense counsel to make a reasonable return for their time and overhead.

The next chapter discusses the role of the Judge.

#27

The Judge (Also The Arbitrator): You Can Play A Leading Role In Ending This Game

You have many opportunities to help end this costly game. You are in a position of authority to help end it. You can do a lot to persuade the litigants, their attorneys and the insurance companies to understand how they lose by playing this game.

You will find throughout this book information you can use to persuade the litigants, attorneys and insurance companies to end this game. You can show them how it is in their best interest to do so.

In addition, this will help you reduce your docket.

The next chapter identifies the sponsor of the game.

#28

You The Law Maker Regulator: Sponsor This Game

If you examine the states that have had rate regulation the longest, you will find that regulating insurance rates doesn't help obtain insurance coverage for less. Take a close look at Massachusetts and New Jersey.

Their policyholders especially automobile are paying the highest rates in the nation and a large percentage are in the assigned risk pool. In New Jersey, the state has run up billions of dollars in losses. You want the insurance companies to reimburse your state for the losses you incurred as a result of imprudent regulation. You threaten insurance companies with cancelling their other lines if they do not subsidize your losses from automobile insurance. Do you really think this is fair?

For years, large insurance companies wanted to be able to advertise that they did business in all states. As a result, from profits in other states, they subsidized New Jersey, Massachusetts and other states. Insurers cannot do this anymore. As more states regulate insurance rates and roll back premiums, fewer insurers can divert funds from policyholders in one state to subsidize drivers in other states. It isn't fair to continue to expect the insured in other states to subsidize your drivers. Are you proud that you have converted auto insurance into a cost plus operation?

All that you need do is free your insurance companies of rate regulation and let old fashioned American competition and markct forces take over. You know this will bring down the insurance rates especially automobile to reasonable levels.

Equally important, drivers will be able to choose their own insurance carriers more freely.

When only a few states regulated insurance rates, insurers could play your game. You could claim you are saving your drivers a lot of money on their insurance. It was considered good politics. When the voters in your state realize that regulation is not saving them money but costing them dearly, it has become bad politics.

When policyholders in regulated states realize that you are sponsoring this 96 Billion Dollar Game, they will rebel against this expensive game that costs them so dearly. Be in the lead, move to lift rate regulation and let old fashion American competition become the order of the day.

See Chapter 15 - Public Officials Who Promise You Lower Insurance Premiums Through Rate Regulation Are A Major Cause Of The Game.

In the next chapter, we examine how the 96 Billion Dollar Game can come to an end.

#29

The Final Play: Information, Marketing And Economics Can Force An End To Non-Productive Litigation

Take heart, we do not need new laws or new regulations to eliminate this expensive non-productive game. We need you to use the information that has been outlined throughout this book. You and the other players and social forces will cause the demise of the 96 Billion Dollar Game.

The reason is simple. It is in the best financial interest of all the players that the game comes to an end. When each player recognizes how costly the game is to him, he will take steps to take control. This book tells each of you how you got in the game, what the game is about and how you can take control.

You represent most of the adult population of the United States plus the many businesses and governmental units. Collectively, you have power to end this costly game.

APPENDIX

The costs used throughout this book are based on various industry sources and publications. This appendix shows how some of those costs were calculated.

#3 General Background

Number of Lawsuits

In many instances throughout this text, the cost of an item is reported on a per lawsuit basis. To accurately project the total cost several years down the road, both the cost itself and the number of lawsuits to which it applies must be calculated.

The estimate of the number of lawsuits resolved in 1991 is based on the 1985 Rand Corporation study, Cost and Compensation Paid in Tort Litigation.

Using reports from the National Center for State Courts and the Administrative Offices of the United States Courts, Rand reported that there were 911,000 tort lawsuits filed in 1985 in both State and Federal courts of general jurisdiction. Slightly fewer, 866,000 were terminated in the same year, 461,000 of these were automobile cases and 405,000 involved other torts.

Rand also reported that the number of filings was increasing at a rate of 3.9 percent annually. This growth rate was reported again in their 1990 annual report.

Applying the 3.9 percent growth rate to the number of cases, we can project 1,146,070 tort cases filed in 1991 and 1,089,460 cases terminated. The following table shows the annual increases.

1991 LAWSUIT FILINGS AND TERMINATIONS

Year	Filing		Termination	
	auto	non-auto	auto	non-auto
1985	485,000	426,000	461,000	405,000
1986	503,915	442,614	478,979	420,795
1987	523,567	459,876	497,659	437,206
1988	543,987	477,811	517,068	454,257
1989	565,203	496,446	537,234	471,973
1990	587,245	515,807	558,186	490,380
1991	**610,147**	**535,923**	**579,955**	**509,505**

In 1990, The National Center for State Courts and the Administrative Office of the United States Courts issued a report, because courts categorize, report and handle civil lawsuits differently and tort is only one small component of the civil court caseload in this country, it is difficult to repeat Rand's calculations.

#4 The Opening Bet: Insurers Gamble 40% Of Your Premiums

LEGAL DEFENSE FEES

Insurance Services Office

The ISO study, Legal Defense: A Large and Growing Insurance Cost, reported that attorney and witness fees for legal defense totaled $11.8 billion in 1988 and increased 16 percent annually between 1978 and 1988.

Since Workers' Compensation is included in the ISO study, but is not part of this examination, the $1.3 billion spent for defense in Workers' Compensation cases is excluded, bringing the total for auto liability, multi-peril, general liability and medical malpractice to $10.5 billion in 1988.

Applying 16 percent annual growth to the 1988 cost, the 1991 cost of legal defense is estimated to be $16 billion.

Rand Corporation Data

Legal defense costs were also studied in the 1985 report Cost and Compensation Paid in Tort Litigation by the Rand Corporation. In this study, Rand looked at two sets of data to determine the cost of litigation. The first was from a University of Wisconsin lawsuit survey and the second was from the insurance industry.

From the University of Wisconsin data, Rand reported the 1985 cost of legal defense and other fees to be $4,900 for each auto claim and $8,500 for each non-auto claim.

Rand also reported that costs for auto claims increased 6.3 percent annually and costs for non-auto claims increased 15 percent annually.

The second estimate of allocated loss and adjustment expense in 1991 takes Rand's University of Wisconsin data on costs and projects it using Rand growth figures.

	AUTO	NON-AUTO
Per case 1985, Rand		
Growth	$ 4,900	$ 8,500
Per case 1991	6.3%	15%
Terminations 1991	$ 7,070	19,661
Total	$579,955	509,505
	$4,100,281,850	$10,017,377,805

Using the insurance industry data for another projection, Rand estimated that $1.05 billion was spent handling auto and $3.68 billion for non-auto claims in 1985. Dividing these totals by the number of cases terminated in 1985, we can deduce that insurance companies spent $2,278 for each auto claim and $9,086 for each non-auto claim in 1985.

The next projection of allocated loss adjustment expense uses Rand's insurance industry data and annual increase factor.

	AUTO	NON-AUTO
Per case 1985, Rand	$ 2,278	$9,806
Growth	6.3% (p 50)	15%(p 57)
Per case 1991	$ 3,287	22,682
Terminations 1991	579,955	509,505
Total	$1,906,312,085	$11,556,515,984

Between these two estimates, Rand data updated to 1991 puts the cost of legal defense at $13.5 billion and $14.1 billion.

Because the ISO study is the most recent data, $16 billion is used as the estimate of Legal Defense Costs.

OPERATING EXPENSES/UNALLOCATED LOSS ADJUSTMENT EXPENSE

ISO Data

In 1988, the ISO publication on legal defense costs reported that unallocated loss adjustment expense totaled $7 billion. However, since many claims are settled without lawsuits and since this estimate includes Workers' Compensation, only a portion of this $7 billion can be blamed on litigation.

According to the 1991 Aggregates and Averages published by A.M. Best, losses for all personal injury lines totalled $60 billion in 1989. Based on the ratio of losses to premiums earned between 1981 and 1990, $74 billion in losses can be expected in 1991.

Applying the 9.9 percent expense from the ISO study to 1991 losses indicates that $7.4 billion will be spent in unallocated loss adjustment expense in 1991 for personal injury lines only.

Since we know how many cases enter litigation, we can use these percentages to estimate how much of the unallocated costs are attributable to litigation. According to the All-Industry Research Advisory Council (AIRAC) report, Compensation for Automobile Injuries in the United States, 18.1 percent of all automobile claims enter litigation. According to the ISO, 25.7 percent of all commercial claims excluding medical malpractice enter litigation. Since there are about the same number of commercial and automobile lawsuits filed each year, we can assume an average of 21.9 percent of all claims enter litigation. Therefore, cases in litigation account for at least 21.9 percent of the $7.4 billion in unallocated costs or $1.6 billion.

Rand Corporation Data

Rand estimated that unallocated loss adjustment expense was $866 per case in 1985. Using the same annual growth rates used to update allocated costs, the following table projects the 1991 unallocated loss adjustment expense. The total unallocated insurance expense in 1991 from updated Rand projections is $1,744,902,310.

	AUTO	NON-AUTO
Per case 1985	$ 866	$ 866
Growth	6.3%	15%
Per case 1991	$ 1,249	$2,003
Terminations 1991	579,955	509,505
Total	$1,906,312,085	$11,556,515,984

COMPENSATION PAID

In order to measure how much compensation grows due to inflation, it is first necessary to determine the compensation paid to injured plaintiffs in 1991.

Rand Corporation

In determining how much compensation was paid in the average personal injury claim, Rand tapped into two sources, a survey by the University of Wisconsin and insurance industry data.

From the University of Wisconsin, Rand reported that compensation paid per lawsuit in 1985 averaged $26,700 for auto cases and $31,600 for non-auto cases.

According to the insurance industry data gathered by Rand, $8.1 billion was paid in auto compensation and $12.6 billion in non-auto compensation. Using Rand's report 461,000 auto terminations and 405,000 non-auto terminations, we can deduce that according to the insurance industry data, compensation paid per lawsuit was $17,570 for auto and $31,111 for non-auto.

Rand also reported that compensation in automobile claims were growing 12 percent annually and non-auto compensation was increasing 17 percent annually.

Jury Verdict Research, Inc. analyzes the size of verdicts, and its 1991 Current Award Trends (CAT) reports that verdicts have increased an average of 8.17 percent annually since 1963.

Because of the different estimates of 1985 compensation and growth rates, the total cost of compensation in 1991 will be estimated using each of these cost and growth figures.

The first estimate of compensation paid in 1991 takes Rand's University of Wisconsin data on compensation paid per case and projects it using both Rand and JVR growth figures.

ESTIMATE #1

	AUTO	NON-AUTO
Per case 1985	$26,700(p22)	$31,600(p33)
Annual growth	Rand 12%-JVR 8.17% (p23)(91 CAT)	Rand 17%-JVR 8.17 (p33) (91 CAT)
Per case 1991	$52,701-$42,177	$81,059-$50,621

The second estimate of compensation paid in 1991 takes Rand's insurance industry data on compensation paid per case and projects it using both RAND and JVR growth figures.

ESTIMATE #2

	AUTO	NON-AUTO
Per case 1985, Rand	$17,570	$31,111
Annual growth	Rand 12%-JVR 8.17% (p23)(91 CAT)	Rand 17%-JVR 8.17 (p33) (91 CAT)
Per case 1991	$34,680-$28,146	$79,805-$49,837

ISO Data - Commercial

According to the ISO study, Claim File Data Analysis, the average payment for a commercial lawsuit in 1987 was $37,009. According to Current Award Trends by JVR, verdicts have increased 8.17 percent a year since 1963. Increasing 8.17 percent annually, the average payment will go up to $50,668 in 1991.

AIRAC Data - Automobile

According to the 1987 All-Industry Research Advisory Council (AIRAC) study, Compensation for Automobile Injuries in the United States, average compensation in 1987 for automobile cases in which lawsuits were filed was $18,343. Updating these amounts using JVR's 8.17 percent annual growth rate indicates that the average compensation in 1991 will be $25,113.

Compensation Paid

Because the ISO and AIRAC data are the most recent estimates, they are used as the average 1991 compensation.

INCREASED COSTS DUE TO ANNUAL GROWTH IN

Verdict Size

Burgeoning medical costs and inflation push the size of verdicts up every year. If there is any delay in making payment whether through settlement or verdict, this increase affects the payment.

ISO Data - Commercial Claims

Using the above compensation figures, we can determine how much the value of an average claim will grow over two years, which is the average length of time a claim is in litigation, according to the ISO.

Year	8.17% Increase	Total Value
Base		$50,688
1	4,141	54,829
2	8,621	59,309
3	13,467	64,154
4	18,708	69,396
5	24,378	75,065

6	30,511	81,198
7	37,145	87,832
8	44,321	95,008
9	52,083	102,770

Rand - Auto Compensation

In 1985,Cost and Compensation in Tort Litigation reported that automobile claims averaged 16 months in litigation. The increasing criminal docket, which takes priority over civil cases clearly indicates that the present delay is greater than 16 months. However, to be conservative, we will use the 1985 figure.

The following table use these figures to determine how much the value of an average automobile claim will grow over time.

Year	8.17% Increase	Total Value
Base		$25,113
1	2,052	54,829
1.33	2,812	27,925
2	4,261	29,384
3	6,662	31,785
4	9,259	34,381
5	12,068	37,191
6	15,106	40,229
7	18,393	43,516
8	21,948	47,071
9	25,794	50,917

#5 Policyholders: May Never Play A Hand, But They Pick Up The Tab

Routine Litigation Costs

In Cost and Compensation Paid in Tort Litigation, Rand estimated that in 1985, defendant's time spent on lawsuit related activity was worth $1,530 to $2,474 for each auto case and $5,892 to $6,034 for each non-auto case. The low estimate is based on minimum wage and the high estimate is based on the hourly rate of the highest wage earner in the household.

The total value of defendants' time in 1985 was estimated to be $2.5 to $3.5 billion.

Rand provides no increase in these values for use in projecting. They use 1979 dollars, "adjusted to 1985 dollars". To estimate the 1991, cost we apply the average increase in the CPI between 1985 and 1990, which is 4.0 percent. To apply this inflation growth figure on a per case basis, we update the per case cost then multiply them by the estimated number of cases terminated.

	AUTO	NON-AUTO
1985, per case	1,530	2,474
Updated at 4% yearly	5,892	6,034
No. of term. 1991	1,936	3,130

Defense person costs	1,037,546,928	1,677,438,990
	4,323,564,525	4,427,956,425

This puts the total value of defendants' time between $5,361,111,453 and 6,105,395,415.

#6 Victim Again: The Injured Lose $9 Billion

LITIGATION COSTS INCURRED BY PLAINTIFFS

Rand Corporation

To file, develop and present a plaintiff's case, the plaintiff and his attorney must pay filing fees, expert witness consultation, testimony charges and court reporter fees for depositions and transcripts. These are referred to as out-of-pocket expenses. These expenses are often paid by the plaintiff attorney, who is reimbursed once settlement is reached. If the route chosen for resolution were not litigation, none or only a small portion of these costs would be incurred.

In Cost and Compensation, Rand reported that legal costs other than attorney fees, "accounted for 10 percent or less of the total legal fees and expenses incurred by the plaintiff".

Since commercial plaintiffs will pay an average of $15,707 in legal fees and expenses, 31 percent of the total compensation expenses will total about $1,570 per case. At $1,570 for 579,955 cases, commercial plaintiffs spend $.9 billion on out-of-pocket legal expenses.

With automobile compensation of $25,113 (AIRAC) the out-of-pocket totals $779 per case and $.5 billion for the 579,995 automobile plaintiffs.

Between commercial and automobile claims, this estimate puts out-of-pocket litigation expenses at $1.4 billion. However, since these out-of-pocket expenses are often reimbursed before the attorney takes his share, in effect the attorney absorbs about one-third of the expense, leaving $.9 billion on the plaintiffs' shoulders.

These out-of-pocket expenses are most likely much too low by today's experience.

Philip J. Hermann, with the assistance of Jury Verdict Research, Inc.

Philip J. Hermann also studied the cost of litigation and its results are reported in the manual Better, Earlier Settlements Through Economic Leverage. From the cost accounting of representative personal injury cases, the manual's tables project the various costs of litigation based on the value of the case.

Using the tables in that manual, the following table estimates the out-of-pocket costs of these average cases. The costs incurred prior to filing a lawsuit are not included, since they are not part of the litigation process and would be incurred even if a lawsuit were not filed.

OUT-OF-POCKET COSTS

	Compensation	Out-of-pocket
Auto	$25,113	$2,774
Non-auto	$50,668	$4,056
Average	$37,901	$3,415

Since these are the costs to litigate to a verdict, and most cases are settled before a trial, I estimate that on average, resolution is about halfway between the filing of a lawsuit and delivery of the verdict. Therefore, we use about half of the above cited costs as the overall average for litigated cases. Accordingly, average out-of-pocket costs will be about $2,000 per case or a total of $2.2 billion.

Out-of-pocket expenses come off the top of all settlements and plaintiff verdicts decreasing the injured parties' share to $1.5 billion.

Litigation expenses are far more than just out-of-pocket costs, but they are absorbed by the attorney in the form of salaries for associates, paralegals and the expenses of running the law firm.

PLAINTIFF PERSONAL EXPENSES

The plaintiff also has personal expenses above and beyond these litigation expenses. When he has to meet with his attorneys or attend proceedings, he often has to take time off work and loses wages.

Rand Corporation Study

In 1985, Cost and Compensation Paid in Tort Litigation estimated that plaintiffs' incurred $1,668 to $2,031 in lost wages per non-auto case. As with the defendant's time, the value of the plaintiff's time is increased 4.0 percent annually the average CPI increase between 1985 and 1990. When updated to 1991, these grow to $2,110 - $2,570 per case or a total of $1.1 to $1.3 billion. However, there is a strong indication that the personal costs are much higher in the commercial cases.

The value of time spent in auto cases totalled $378 to $678 per case in 1985. In 1991, the cost per case is estimated at $478 to $858 or a total of $.3 billion to $.5 billion.

Personal expenses account for $1.4 to $1.8 billion of the total litigation bill.

#7 Raising The Bet: Plaintiff Attorneys Risk $7.5 Billion

In examining the bottom line of the plaintiff attorney, Better, Earlier Settlements presented spreadsheet analysis of several cases, showing how the costs incurred at different stages of litigation affected the attorneys hourly return. The following spreadsheets present analysis of plaintiff attorney income in $10,000 and $80,000 cases with the partner performing half of the litigation functions and the paralegal and associate doing the rest.

Establishing Plaintiff Attorney Profit and Loss

Case 1A:
Rear-end Collision, Lumbar Strain
73% Plaintiff Recovery Probability

50% Partner Hours
$10,000 Probable Verdic

HOURS PARTNER 50% ASSOCIATE 40% PARALEGAL 10%	PRIOR TO SUIT	TO PRETRIAL	TRIAL PREPARATION	TRIAL TO VERDICT	PLAINTIFF VERDICT	DEFENSE VERDICT	POST TRIAL
Probable Verdict Amount					10,000	0	NA
Basic Settlement Value	3,746	3,746	3,746	3,746			
Out-Of-Pocket Costs	(200)	(300)	(1,380)	(1,505)	(1,505)	(1,505)	
Net Recovery	3,546	3,446	2,366	2,241	8,495	(1,505)	
Partner Hours	10	20	30	40	40	40	
25% FEE	886	861	591	560	2,124	0	
Time & Overhead	(1,188)	(2,376)	(3,564)	(4,752)	(4,752)	(4,752)	
NET FEE	(302)	(1,515)	(2,973)	(4,192)	(2,628)	(6,257)	
Partner Hourly Return	(30)	(76)	(99)	(105)	(66)	(156)	
33% FEE	1,182	1,148	788	747	2,831	0	
Time & Overhead	(1,188)	(2,376)	(3,564)	(4,752)	(4,752)	(4,752)	
NET FEE	(6)	(1,228)	(2,776)	(4,005)	(1,921)	(6,257)	
Partner Hourly Return	(1)	(61)	(93)	(100)	(48)	(156)	

Establishing Plaintiff Attorney Profit and Loss

50% FEE	1,773	1,723	1,183	1,120	4,248	0	
Time & Overhead	(1,188)	(2,376)	(3,564)	(4,752)	(4,752)	(4,752)	
NET FEE	585	(653)	(2,381)	(3,632)	(505)	(6,257)	
Partner Hourly Return	58	(33)	(79)	(91)	(13)	(156)	

FUTURE VALUE: 8.375% INTEREST SETTLEMENT VS VERDICT	BASE VALUE	YEAR 1	YEAR 2	YEAR 3	YEAR 5	YEAR 7	YEAR 9
25% NET FEE							
SETTLEMENT PRIOR TO SUIT	(302)						
PLAINTIFF VERDICT	(2,628)						
w/27% Defense Verdict Probability	(1,919)						
33% NET FEE							
SETTLEMENT PRIOR TO SUIT	(6)						
PLAINTIFF VERDICT	(1,921)						
w/27% Defense Verdict Probability	(1,402)						
50% NET FEE							
SETTLEMENT PRIOR TO SUIT	585	634	687	744	874	1,027	1,206
PLAINTIFF VERDICT	(505)						
w/27% Defense Verdict Probability	(368)						

Establishing Plaintiff Attorney Profit and Loss

Case 4A:
Pedestrian Accident, Pelvic Fracture
48% Plaintiff Recovery Probability

50% Partner Hours
$80,000 Probable Verdi

HOURS PARTNER 50% ASSOCIATE 40% PARALEGAL 10%	PRIOR TO SUIT	TO PRETRIAL	TRIAL PREPARATION	TRIAL TO VERDICT	PLAINTIFF VERDICT	DEFENSE VERDICT	POST TRIAL
Probable Verdict Amount					80,000	0	80,00
Basic Settlement Value	34,951	34,951	34,951	34,951			
Out-Of-Pocket Costs	(1,500)	(1,980)	(5,065)	(5,970)	(5,970)	(5,970)	(7,90
Net Recovery	33,451	32,971	29,886	28,981	74,030	(5,970)	72,09
Partner Hours	20	40	65	90	90	90	11
25% FEE	8,363	8,243	7,472	7,245	18,508	0	18,02
Time & Overhead	(2,376)	(4,752)	(7,722)	(10,692)	(10,692)	(10,692)	(13,66
NET FEE	5,987	3,491	(250)	(3,447)	7,816	(16,662)	4,36
Partner Hourly Return	299	87	(4)	(38)	87	(185)	3
33% FEE	11,149	10,989	9,961	9,659	24,674	0	24,02
Time & Overhead	(2,376)	(4,752)	(7,722)	(10,692)	(10,692)	(10,692)	(13,66
NET FEE	8,773	6,237	2,239	(1,033)	13,982	(16,662)	10,36
Partner Hourly Return	439	156	34	(11)	155	(185)	9

Establishing Plaintiff Attorney Profit and Loss

50% FEE	16,726	16,486	14,943	14,491	37,015	0	36,048
Time & Overhead	(2,376)	(4,752)	(7,722)	(10,692)	(10,692)	(10,692)	(13,662)
NET FEE	14,350	11,734	7,221	3,799	26,323	(16,662)	22,386
Partner Hourly Return	717	293	111	42	292	(185)	195

FUTURE VALUE: 8.375% INTEREST SETTLEMENT VS VERDICT	BASE VALUE	YEAR 1	YEAR 2	YEAR 3	YEAR 5	YEAR 7	YEAR 9
25% NET FEE							
SETTLEMENT PRIOR TO SUIT	5,987	6,488	7,032	7,621	8,950	10,512	12,347
PLAINTIFF VERDICT	7,816						
w/48% Defense Verdict Probability	4,064						
33% NET FEE							
SETTLEMENT PRIOR TO SUIT	8,773	9,508	10,304	11,167	13,116	15,405	18,094
PLAINTIFF VERDICT	13,982						
w/48% Defense Verdict Probability	7,271						
50% NET FEE							
SETTLEMENT PRIOR TO SUIT	14,350	15,551	16,854	18,265	21,453	25,197	29,594
PLAINTIFF VERDICT	26,323						
w/48% Defense Verdict Probability	13,688						

#10 Hoyle's Rules: Billion Dollars With Final Say

Court Costs

According to Rand Corporation's Cost and Compensation in Tort Litigation total court expenditure for tort cases in 1985, including salaries and certain portions of fringe benefits, accounting, construction and operation was $1/2 billion. This broke down to $535 per state court case and $1,948 per case filed in federal court less $75 per case to avoid double counting the amount paid by litigating parties. Rand indicated that state court expenditure increased 31 percent from 1982 to 1985. USDC expenditure increased 11 percent over that three year period.

To update 1985 expenditure to 1991, we will double the increase, since it was double the time period. Since we are doubling the growth projection, we will also double the deduction for costs paid by litigants to $150 per case.

	State	USDC
1985 expenses per case	$ 535	$1,948
Increase from 1985-91	62%	22%
1991 expenses per case	$ 867	2,377
-$150 for litig. payments	$ 717	2,227
Cases terminated in 1985	827,000	39,000

Annual growth	3.9%	5.0%
Cases terminated in 1991	1,040,396	52,264
Total court expenses, 1991	$745,944,573	116,391,928

The total state and USDC expenditure in 1991 is estimated to be $862 million.

Jury Costs

The court expenditure is just a portion of what it cost to process a case through the court system. For each case that reaches trial, jurors must be called in to serve. The court expenses just outlined will cover court processing costs, but the cost of juries is not included in Rand's estimate. While it may seem like a minor issue, the cost of paying for the jurors' time quickly mounts.

The report A Comparison of the Performance of Eight- and Twelve-Person Juries, by the National Center for State Courts (NCSC) provides data to help project the total cost of tort juries. Since all of the estimates in this book are on the conservative side to avoid overstating the cost of litigation, we will project costs based on eight-person juries in all tort trials.

Since we know there was approximately 1,089,460 lawsuits terminated and the National Center for State Courts also reports that 2.94 percent of the tort disposition are jury trials, we can project that 32,030 tort trials were held un 1991.

Jury fees

The NCSC reported that most eight-person juries were selected from a panel of 22 people and each person spent one day going through the selection process. Trials averaged three days, eight jurors and two alternates were required. In the final phase, the eight jurors spent an average of two days in deliberations. This means each trial required 68 individual juror trial days.

In another report, the NCSC indicated the average daily juror fee for each state, as well as who paid the fee. In 74 percent of the states, the local or state government pays the jurors and the average rate is $14 per day. In the remaining state, the losing party in a civil suit pays jurors fees through the court costs.

The portion of juror fees paid by litigants are not added here since they were taken into account when we talked about the plaintiff's and defendant's costs.

Using these figures, the following table calculates the juror fees paid by the government.

68	total juror days per trial
x 32,030	jury trials
2,178,040	juror trial days
x 74%	states in which the local or state government pays
1,611,750	juror trial days in states in which the local or state government pays
x $ 14	average daily payment by government
$22,564,495	total jury fees paid by government

This estimate only takes into account the time each juror or potential juror actually spends on a specific tort case. In most jurisdictions, potential jurors spend a couple weeks on jury duty, whether or not they are selected for a case. Adding the cost of these jurors in waiting would increase this figure substantially.

Wc have no way of allocating these additional costs, but just to see how high the cost might be, assume that the 22 jurors called for each tort trial are serving a two-week term. For each of the 30,030 trials, there would be 220 juror trial days or a total of 6,606,600 days. At $14 each, the bill would be $92.5 million.

Travel Reimbursement

The same group of people who receive jury pay from state and local governments receive mileage reimbursement. The average rate is 14 cents a mile. While the average distance traveled by a juror is not known using a 30 mile round-trip will provide some insight into the mileage cost.

$.14	average per mile reimbursement for round-trip, paid by state/local government
x 30	round-trip estimate
$4.20	per juror per day
1,611,750	juror trial days in state in which the government pays travel reimbursement
$6,769,350	

Juror's Lost Income

Only six percent of the jurors in the NCSC study reported that they lost income during jury duty. The average reported loss was $60. The remaining jurors were either paid their regular salary or were not employed, such as homemakers or retirees.

The following calculates the jurors' lost income. Unlike the two previous categories, this calculation is based on the total number of jury trial days, not only those paid for by the government.

2,178,040	juror trial days
x 6%	percentage of jurors who reported lost income
130,682	juror trial days for which jurors lost income
x $60	average reported lost income
$7,840,944	jurors' lost income

Employers' Cost

While the remaining 94 percent of jurors did not lose money, the employers who paid their salaries did. With the average daily wage of a non-farm worker in the U.S. is $70, the following table calculates the total cost of wages paid to employees while on jury duty.

2,178,040	juror trial days
x 94%	percent of employers who pay employees while on jury duty
1,611,749	juror trial days paid for by employers
x $70	average daily wage of non-farm worker (U.S. Department of Labor)
$112,822,430	employers' cost

#21 Policyholders: The Winning Hand Can Be Yours

Varying Size Premiums-Automobile Insurance

The purpose of this appendix to Chapter 21 is to disclose and detail the varying rates charged for automotive liability insurance by the various companies underwriting these policies.

The State of Ohio insurance department survey covered various cities and other areas in Ohio. By writing or calling the department of insurance in your state you can obtain their latest Shopper's Guide to Auto Insurance.

The final results of the Ohio survey show the significant savings that can be achieved by shopping around for insurance. Similar savings may well be obtainable in other states.

IMPORTANT NOTE: The policy and the premiums charged by insurance companies may change from time to time. In underwriting and setting premiums for automobile risks, so many driving and family factors are involved that different agents in the same company and for the same locality on the same day may due to different impressions, misunderstandings or mistake make vastly different premium quotations. Some of these may be changed by the company's underwriting department. For this reason no reader should draw the conclusion on these observations and on these quotations that the various companies reported herein are high or low premium underwriters. **The important conclusion that should be drawn is that by comparison shopping, you can save substantially.**

CLEVELAND

Prices for drivers living inside city limits. Prices are lower in Cleveland suburbs (SEE PARMA).
(These companies insure a total of 103,774 cars in Cleveland.)

All Drivers: Insuring 1989 Chevrolet Celebrity (4 door), driven to and from work (10 miles each way); new customer with the company but previously insured by another company; priced before qualifying for any discounts; all but "Driver C" have had no tickets within the past 3 years.

Insured Drivers

A: Age 22; single female; no driving age dependents; (may be higher for single male).
B: Age 30; married couple; no driving age dependents.
C: Age 30; married couple; two speeding tickets in the past year.
**Drivers over 30: use "A" or "B". There should be little change in price.
D: Age 40; married couple; 17 year old daughter with driver training.

PRICE RANGES

Driver	A	B	C	D
High	5584	3591	3870	6620
Low	709	567	586	752
Average	1947	1360	1733	2270

Insurance Coverage:

Liability

- Bodily Injury: $50,000/$100,000
- Medical Payments: $5,000
- Property Damage: $25,000
- Uninsured/Underinsured Motorist: $50,000/$100,000

Physical Damage

- Comprehensive: $100 deductible
- Collision: $200/$250 deductible (varies among companies)

COMPANY NAME	DRIVER A	DRIVER B	DRIVER C	DRIVER D
Aetna C & S	N/A	N/A	N/A	N/A
Affirm	N/A	N/A	N/A	N/A
Affirm Adv Tier	N/A	N/A	N/A	N/A
All America	N/A	N/A	N/A	N/A
Allstate Indem	N/A	567	N/A	N/A
Allstate Ins	N/A	582	N/A	N/A
Am Econ	N/A	586	N/A	752
Am Empl	N/A	595	N/A	899
Am F & C	N/A	620	N/A	941
Am Indem	709	626	N/A	943
Am Natl Gen	813	634	N/A	948
Am Natl P & C	814	654	N/A	951
Am Select	832	658	N/A	977
Am St Pref	832	685	N/A	996
Am States	832	695	N/A	1014
Amerisure	832	695	N/A	1016
Amica Mut	863	695	N/A	1038
Assoc Indem	868	695	N/A	1081
Assur Co. Of Am	870	708	N/A	1081
Atlanta Cas	886	708	N/A	1146
Atlantic Mut Ins	897	716	N/A	1148
Auto Club	931	722	N/A	1156
Auto Ins of Hd	940	770	N/A	1172
Auto-Owners	975	780	N/A	1178
Beacon	1008	788	N/A	1191
Bkrs & Ship	1013	818	N/A	1191
Buckeye St	1033	821	N/A	1208
Capl Enterpr	1035	826	N/A	1208
Castle Ins	1056	829	N/A	1208

Celina	1066	847	N/A	1208
Cent Indem	1082	852	N/A	1237
Cent Ins	1110	865	N/A	1279
Charter Oak	1156	867	N/A	1286
Cinti Cas	1174	867	N/A	1288
Cinti Equ	1178	873	N/A	1304
Cinti Indem	1191	884	N/A	1328
Cinti Ins	1214	892	N/A	1364
Col Ins of CA	1224	900	N/A	1388
Col Penn	1224	907	N/A	1391
Com Union	1249	915	N/A	1428
Consolidated	1262	920	N/A	1437
Cont Ins	1348	946	N/A	1438
Coronet	1350	948	N/A	1459
Coventry	1363	960	N/A	1476
Dairyland	1364	966	N/A	1484
Dixie	1364	966	N/A	1522
Eagle Am	1368	970	N/A	1528
Econ F & C	1379	1009	N/A	1528
Econ Pref	1389	1012	N/A	1558
Electric	1393	1012	N/A	1566
Erie	1402	1014	N/A	1569
Farmers	1438	1016	N/A	1579
Fed Kemper	1452	1023	N/A	1580
Fed Kemper KAP	1452	1025	N/A	1600
Federal	1481	1026	N/A	1644
FFIC	1481	1026	N/A	1645
Fld & Guar	1482	1052	N/A	1652

COMPANY NAME	DRIVER A	DRIVER B	DRIVER C	DRIVER D
Frst Natl of Am	2073	1616	2029	2312
Geico Gen	1224	867	N/A	1081
Gen Accident	1962	1476	1476	2803
Germn Mut	2042	1454	N/A	2792
Globe Am	2808	2750	3069	3627
Globe Indem P	886	634	634	1038
Globe Indem SP	814	586	586	948
Gov Empl	1224	867	N/A	1081
Grange Mut Cas	940	828	1574	1566
Great Northern	832	695	832	1208
Hamilton	N/A	1217	N/A	2426
Harleysville	1033	948	948	1288
Hartford Cas	2144	1666	2194	2212
Hartford Fire	1836	1428	1878	1894
Hastings	1828	1158	N/A	2030
Heritage	1758	1124	1377	1685
Home	1066	829	N/A	1645
Horace Mann	5584	3591	3591	5418
Illinois Nat	3252	2472	2560	4590
Indiana	2189	1519	1787	2591
Ins Co of OH	1750	1014	1214	1686
Insura – Plus	2186	1396	N/A	2546
Insura – Prem	2221	1327	N/A	2587
KY Gen	1174	818	1079	1889
Keystone	1389	1052	2457	1364
Leader Nat	1824	1548	1548	2588
Liberty	2046	1651	1748	2169
Libty Mut F	1575	1178	N/A	1696

Ltg Rod Mut	2922	1526	N/A	2606
Lumb Mut Cas	1350	708	1440	1580
Md Cas	2302	1670	1670	2860
Merch of NH	1262	915	915	1146
Merchants Mut	1717	1241	1241	1558
Meridian	813	654	979	943
Meritplan	1008	708	1052	1172
Metro P & C	1842	1456	1694	2354
MI Millers	1946	1234	N/A	2328
MIC	1482	1075	1075	1437
MICO	3036	2528	2528	6620
Midwest Mut	4966	3360	3360	5322
Midwestern	1588	1104	N/A	2264
Milw Guard	1348	920	N/A	1522
Milw Mut	2156	1230	N/A	1778
Motorists	2098	1009	N/A	2646
N Am Spec	870	567	623	998
National	3506	2800	3190	3098
Natl Fire	2727	1911	N/A	2890
Natl Mut	1742	1138	1138	2114
Natl Surety	3539	2274	2274	4065
Natnwd Gen	1363	946	N/A	1279
Natnwd Mut	1516	1078	N/A	1428
Natnwd Mut F	1364	970	N/A	1286
Natnwd P & C	2196	1562	N/A	2071
Newark Ins	1452	1026	1026	1706
NW NTL Cas	2560	1646	1961	2076
Ohio Cas	2872	N/A	1752	N/A
Ohio Frmers	2070	1368	1368	2597

COMPANY NAME	DRIVER A	DRIVER B	DRIVER C	DRIVER D
Ohio Sec	N/A	N/A	2866	N/A
Owners	N/A	1368	1368	2448
PA Gen	1578	1181	N/A	2224
Phoenix	N/A	1427	N/A	N/A
Pref Abst	1829	1329	N/A	2052
Pref Mut	1013	685	N/A	1237
Pref Risk	2443	1949	N/A	2772
Princ Cas	1488	780	1526	1016
Prog Cas	2804	2546	2646	3426
Prog Spec	2538	2314	2400	3098
Pru Gen	2952	2344	N/A	3054
Pru P & C	1962	1556	N/A	2030
Rep Frank	2308	1665	1665	2308
Rep Mut	2734	2104	2328	3657
Royl Indem	1110	788	788	1304
Royl Ins	1452	1026	1026	1706
Safeco of Am	1608	1254	N/A	1962
Safeco of IL	1604	1132	N/A	1958
Safeguard	868	620	620	1014
Security Natl	1518	966	N/A	1748
Select	1156	847	N/A	1156
Seneca	1178	873	1061	1178
Sentry	2414	1636	1696	2774
Sentry PAYBACK	N/A	1371	N/A	2320
Shelby – Std	2573	1642	N/A	3002
South Car	2184	1569	N/A	2184

State Auto Mut	1942	1078	1078	1878
State Auto P & C	N/A	884	N/A	N/A
State Farm F & C	1402	1114	1402	1459
State Farm Mut	1082	852	N/A	1148
Std Fire	1700	1354	1354	2046
St. Paul Guar	1879	770	630	941
Sun	832	695	832	1208
Superior	4580	2932	3072	5655
Teachers	5357	3096	3096	5781
Transam	2034	1442	1798	2270
Transam Indem	1820	1288	1608	2034
Transam of Am	2368	1678	2090	2642
Travelers	2666	N/A	N/A	3160
Trinity Univ	1698	1076	1076	1956
Unigard	1056	1056	2344	1656
United OH	2094	1142	1656	2744
USAA	897	626	843	951
USAA Cas	1035	722	972	1191
USF&G	2304	1679	1679	2304
Valley Forge	2005	1415	N/A	2126
Vigilant	832	695	832	1208
Wayne Mut	1191	658	1007	1191
West Am	1946	1198	N/A	2446
Western Res	2320	1644	N/A	2910
Westfield	1669	1108	1108	2088
Westfield Natl	1249	821	N/A	1569
Worldwide	975	892	N/A	1484

SMALL TOWN / RURAL AREAS

Companies call this "remainder of state" and use these prices for many locations outside major cities.
(These companies insure a total of 928,243 cars in "Remainder of State".)

All Drivers: Insuring 1989 Chevrolet Celebrity (4 door), driven to and from work (10 miles each way); new customer with the company but previously insured by another company; priced before qualifying for any discounts; all but "Driver C" have had no tickets within the past 3 years.

Insured Drivers

A: Age 22; single female; no driving age dependents; (may be higher for single male).
B: Age 30; married couple; no driving age dependents.
C: Age 30; married couple; two speeding tickets in the past year.
**Drivers over 30: use "A" or "B". There should be little change in price.
D: Age 40; married couple; 17 year old daughter with driver training.

PRICE RANGES

Driver	A	B	C	D
High	1919	1886	1968	3168
Low	426	326	342	497
Average	900	638	819	1054

Insurance Coverage:

Liability

- Bodily Injury: $50,000/$100,000
- Medical Payments: $5,000
- Property Damage: $25,000
- Uninsured/Underinsured Motorist: $50,000/$100,000

Physical Damage

- Comprehensive: $100 deductible
- Collision: $200/$250 deductible (varies among companies)

COMPANY NAME	DRIVER A	DRIVER B	DRIVER C	DRIVER D
Aetna C & S	732	590	N/A	872
Affirm	1460	1304	1393	2054
Affirm Adv Tier	1363	1219	1302	1913
All America	698	468	N/A	772
Allstate Indem	1394	992	1054	1394
Allstate Ins	759	579	N/A	787
Am Econ	813	604	N/A	1021
Am Empl	842	390	N/A	764
Am F & C	N/A	414	N/A	890
Am Indem	889	642	N/A	1014
Am Natl Gen	1216	908	1420	1278
Am Natl P & C	832	620	N/A	874
Am Select	772	536	N/A	1128
Am St Pref	525	389	N/A	540
Am States	1017	756	N/A	1277
Amerisure	932	452	N/A	966
Amica Mut	757	567	567	852
Assoc Indem	1121	750	750	1292
Assur Co. Of Am	768	556	556	1088
Atlanta Cas	1443	1165	1257	1941
Atlantic Mut Ins	606	486	1239	640
Auto Club	868	514	N/A	803
Auto Ins of Hd	898	722	722	1074
Auto-Owners	1000	710	710	1246
Beacon	908	728	728	1336
Bkrs & Ship	1509	1169	1225	1835
Buckeye St	820	576	N/A	942
Capl Enterpr	N/A	594	N/A	N/A
Castle Ins	1002	628	888	1002

Celina	918	606	606	1108
Cent Indem	822	421	602	606
Cent Ins	606	486	1239	640
Charter Oak	N/A	N/A	1155	N/A
Cinti Cas	639	356	356	823
Cinti Equ	721	504	678	1132
Cinti Indem	872	494	494	1054
Cinti Ins	710	399	399	834
Col Penn	1296	838	N/A	1460
Com Union	1096	496	586	952
Consolidated	784	553	646	923
Cont Ins	961	658	880	1156
Coronet	1109	991	1080	1789
Coventry	1628	1258	1372	2256
Dairyland	1860	1344	1560	2436
Dixie	1426	1114	1210	1990
Eagle Am	736	370	446	1072
Econ F & C	738	596	N/A	808
Econ Pref	554	450	N/A	588
Electric	664	459	493	692
Erie	527	407	N/A	552
Farmers	683	457	N/A	867
Fed Kemper	1054	668	1824	1054
Fed Kemper KAP	710	500	N/A	710
Federal	583	496	583	822
FFIC	1454	959	959	1683
Fid & Guar	704	515	N/A	799
Frankenmuth	848	558	N/A	968

COMPANY NAME	DRIVER A	DRIVER B	DRIVER C	DRIVER D
Frst Natl of Am	975	740	915	1085
Geico Gen	782	555	N/A	691
Gen Accident	711	532	532	972
Germn Mut	756	544	N/A	1026
Globe Am	1681	1886	1886	2310
Globe Indem P	608	446	446	704
Globe Indem SP	548	404	404	636
Gov Empl	782	555	N/A	691
Grange Mut Cas	624	552	1066	1042
Great Northern	583	496	583	822
Hamilton	N/A	551	N/A	1076
Harleysville	469	388	388	631
Hartford Cas	886	690	892	912
Hartford Fire	768	600	774	790
Hastings	438	560	N/A	970
Heritage	746	466	569	718
Home	761	583	N/A	1096
Horace Mann	1398	961	961	1362
Illinois Nat	1296	1006	1036	1794
Indiana	800	565	659	943
Ins Co of OH	706	416	494	676
Insura – Plus	741	477	N/A	860
Insura – Prem	750	453	N/A	873
KY Gen	796	558	734	1279
Keystone	648	502	1076	636
Leader Nat	1348	1156	1156	1900
Liberty	895	727	778	946
Libty Mut F	696	529	N/A	747

Ltg Rod Mut	1080	580	N/A	966
Lumb Mut Cas	896	482	952	1052
Md Cas	966	702	702	1356
Merch of NH	695	499	499	734
Merchants Mut	946	673	673	1000
Meridian	567	461	677	653
Meritplan	460	326	480	536
Metro P & C	792	616	738	1026
MI Millers	656	438	N/A	774
MIC	795	571	571	885
MICO	1372	1132	1132	3168
Midwest Mut	1842	1122	1122	2004
Midwestern	710	508	N/A	996
Milw Guard	692	480	N/A	768
Milw Mut	1098	616	N/A	898
Motorists	956	467	N/A	1265
N Am Spec	519	350	381	589
National	1664	1350	1968	1482
Natl Fire	1027	732	N/A	1086
Natl Frmers	637	506	N/A	824
Natl Mut	777	518	518	936
Natl Surety	1919	1265	1265	2228
Natnwd Gen	767	520	N/A	717
Natnwd Mut	857	597	N/A	805
Natnwd Mut F	771	537	N/A	724
Natnwd P & C	1242	865	N/A	1167
Newark Ins	1228	870	870	1440
NW NTL Cas	695	440	520	659
Ohio Cas	1068	N/A	660	N/A

COMPANY NAME	DRIVER A	DRIVER B	DRIVER C	DRIVER D
Ohio Frmers	956	636	636	1198
Ohio Sec	N/A	N/A	974	N/A
Owners	N/A	576	576	1004
PA Gen	573	439	N/A	790
Phoenix	N/A	539	N/A	N/A
Pref Abst	735	536	N/A	824
Pref Mut	638	438	N/A	774
Pref Risk	738	591	N/A	835
Princ Cas	1100	572	1128	749
Prog Cas	1404	1208	1270	1710
Prog Spec	1276	1100	1160	1550
Pru Gen	1098	872	N/A	1134
Pru P & C	728	576	N/A	752
Rep Frank	980	703	703	1119
Rep Mut	1361	1071	1183	1773
Royl Indem	980	688	688	1122
Royl Ins	1228	870	870	1440
Safeco of Am	975	740	915	1085
Safeco of IL	746	516	N/A	904
Safeguard	778	562	562	910
Security Natl	674	436	N/A	774
Select	627	452	N/A	714
Seneca	777	573	687	879
Sentry	906	614	659	995
Sentry PAYBACK	N/A	516	N/A	759
Shelby – Std	898	575	N/A	1045
South Car	898	635	N/A	1029

State Auto Mut	1060	530	530	1056
State Auto P & C	N/A	426	N/A	N/A
State Farm F & C	845	672	845	880
State Farm Mut	696	518	N/A	716
Std Fire	898	722	722	1074
St. Paul Guar	1002	394	342	497
Sun	583	496	583	822
Superior	1748	1143	1194	2122
Teachers	1352	854	854	1445
Transam	864	610	762	966
Transam Indem	702	496	618	782
Transam of Am	912	646	806	1018
Travelers	996	N/A	N/A	1176
Trinity Univ	798	512	512	918
Unigard	426	426	888	642
United OH	790	444	662	1030
USAA	646	456	606	683
USAA Cas	742	523	696	851
USF&G	976	701	701	1114
Valley Forge	767	554	N/A	810
Vigilant	583	496	583	822
Wayne Mut	691	380	581	691
West Am	726	454	N/A	908
Western Res	900	648	N/A	1124
Westfield	769	513	513	930
Westfield Natl	587	393	N/A	732
Worldwide	617	563	N/A	939

Reference Sources

Administrative Office U.S. Courts
1990 Annual Report Of The Director

A. M. Best
Aggregates & Averages:
Property & Casualty 1991 edition
Review, Corporate Changes (insurance companies) March 1988.

ABA Journal
Putting The Rocket In The Docket
October 1990.

Adjustments, by H. Lawrence Ross,
Published by Aldine.

Alliance Of American Insurers
Residual Markets, 1988

Arthur Andersen & Co.
Enterprise Survey, 1989

All-Industry Research Advisory Council:
Automobile Injuries And Their Compensation in the U.S. March 1989.
Compensation Paid In Automobile Injuries In the United States, 1979.

Altman & Weil's Survey Of Law Firm Economics
1989 and 1990.

Bad Faith Actions Against Insurance Companies, Study Of Personal Injury Verdicts, Jury Verdict Research.

Better, Earlier Settlements Through Economic Leverage, by Philip J. Hermann, Legal Information Publications.

Better Settlements Through Leverage, by Philip J. Hermann, Lawyers Cooperative Publishing, Co.

Business Insurance:
The Impact Of Alternatives March 2, 1987.
Self-Insurance January 28, 1991.

Civil Jury As Regulator Of The Litigation Process, by Professor Marc Galanter, University of Chicago. Legal Forum, Volume 1990.

Competition And The Rating Laws: Do They Make A Difference
ABA meeting, January 13, 1989 by
Jean C. Hiestand, V.P. & General Counsel of State Farm Insurance Co.

Current Liability Trends 1991, by Jury Verdict Research.

Current Award Trends 1991 & 1992, Jury Verdict

How To Get Advantageous Settlements, by Philip J. Hermann, Jury Verdict Research.

Injured? How To Get Every Dollar You Deserve, by Philip J. Hermann, Legal Information Publications.

Insurance Information Fact Book 1992.

Insurance Research Council
Trends In Auto Bodily Injury Claims, November 1990

Insurance Service Office (ISO) Claim Data Analysis:
Overview, 1988
Technical Analysis Of Study, 1988
Governmental And Municipal Cost, 1989

ISO Study Legal Defense: A Large And Growing Insurance Cost, 1989.

Legal Negotiation And Settlement, by
Professor Gerald R. Williams, Brigham Young University, West Publishing.

Liability, by Peter Huber

National Association Of Insurance Commissions:
Multi-State Insurance Insolvencies, 1990

National Center For State Courts

Annual Report, 1990 (February 1992).
Letter from Larry L. Sipes, President, April 14, 1992.

National Safety Council, The (1989 Report)

National Underwriter,
The Vehicle Crashes Cost, March 25, 1991.

Newsweek:
The Surge In Self-Insurance, March 7 1988.

Price-Waterhouse

Public Risk Management Society:
The 1987 and 1988 Survey.

RAND Corporation:
Annual Report, 1991
Compensation For Accidental Injuries In The United States, 1991. Annual Report, 1991.
Costs Of The Civil Justice System, 1983.
Cost And Compensation Paid In Tort Litigation, 1985.
Post Trial Adjustment To Jury Awards, 1987.
Statistical Overview, Civil Litigation In The Federal Courts, 1990.

Self-Insurance: Trends And Perspectives
Johnson & Higgins, 1991.

Settled Out Of Court: The Social Process Of Insurance Claims Small Business Survey, 1987.

The Social Process Of Insurance Claims Adjustments
H. Lawrence Ross, Aldine Publishing, 1980.

Tillinghast
Tort Cost Trends: An International Perspective

Tort Cost Trends:
An International Perspective, 1988

Wall Street Journal, The:
Car Insurance Drives Motorists To Brink, February 5, 1988.
What's Driving Auto Insurance Up January 5, 1989.

INDEX

All-Industry Research
    Advisory Council (AIRAC) 29, 33, 135
Awards
    jury 11, 155
Bad Faith
    examples of 44, 45
    improper/inadequate settlements 42
    payment delayed 42
Charts
    Comparison Net Cost At Settlement and Verdict (Chart R) 217
    Comparison Net Cost At Settlement and Verdict (Chart T) 219
    Defense Cost to Plaintiff With Councel (Chart Q) 216
    Defense Costs Direct Settlement (Chart S) 218
    Net Share to Plaintiff Direct Settlement (Chart P) 214
    Net Share to Plaintiff With Counsel (Chart O) 212
    Sample Case (Chart L) 207
Claimant
    definition of 3
Contingent Fees 125
Court Costs 91
Defense Costs
    effect of litigation delay (chart) 185
    chart 184
Defense Counsel
    role of 191
Demand and Offer Study (chart) 140
Demand/Verdict (chart) 146
Employers 93
Fault Compensation System 127
Guaranty Funds
    description of 46
Inflation
    effects of 67
Insurance
    alternative 88
    automobile 28
    cost of 58
    other 28
    personal Injury 28
    policyholders 19
    property/casualty 28
    punitive damage 189
    rates 195
    self-Insurers 23

Insurance Agents (Brokers) 197
Insurance Managers 197
Juror's Lost Income 93
Jury Fees 91
Litigation
- closed claims 35
- cost of 24, 29, 52, 60, 69, 75
- cost to insurance companies 25
- costs for average lawsuit (chart) 76
- defense fees 30
- delay of 61
- effect of delay on attorney's fee (chart) 183
- effects of delay on plaintiff's share (chart) 174
- operating expenses 31
- overpayment to avoid 32
- overpayment to get out of 34
- purpose of 13, 114
- savings on 194
- settlement of 63
- time Span of 66

Malpractice, Legal 80
Marketing To
- plaintiff 178
- plaintiff's attorney 179
- insurance company 183
- self-insurer 183

Negligence System 127
Negotiations
- between attorneys 137
- with adjusters 137
- with Claimant 135

Over-The-Limits Lawsuit 235
Personal Injury
- delays in 117
- delays in lawsuits 99
- Valuation Handbooks 133

Plaintiff 71
- marketing to 178
- marketing to attorney of 178

Policyholders
- business 51
- doctors/hospitals 51
- drivers 51

Probability Tables 159
Punitive Damages 38
- cost of 39
- limits 54, 57
- meaning of 38

Rates
- regulation of 238

Regulatory Interference 149
Reserves 48

Risk Management Consultants 198
Risk Managers 197
Self-insurance 88, 225
Settlement
  investment potential (chart) 64
  value of 170

Settlement Value
  affects of litigation on 161
  affects of time lapse on 163
Time
  between incident and trial (chart) 221
  cost of partner's 77
  effect of 78
Tort
  filings of 97
  definition of 16, 17
Travel 92
Trials
  cost of 94, 96
  expert testimony 95
Verdict
  amounts of 113
  amounts of (chart) 18
  cost to litigate 70
  defense, cost of time 173
  determining value of (chart) 169
  distribution 120
  increased costs of 36
  jury award 11, 155
  post activity 115
  predicting jury 159
  settlement 130
  value of 119, 167
Victimized, Information to Avoid Being 226

OTHER BOOKS BY PHILIP J. HERMANN

To Denny

Hope you enjoy this Book

– Phil